AF800184

I AM A LAW ENFORCEMENT OFFICER. A SOLDIER OF THE LAW.
TO ME IS ENTRUSTED THE HONOR OF THE DEPARTMENT.
I MUST SERVE HONESTLY, FAITHFULLY AND IF NEED BE,
LAY DOWN MY LIFE AS OTHERS HAVE DONE BEFORE ME.

RATHER THAN SWERVE FROM THE PATH OF DUTY,
IT IS MY DUTY TO OBEY THE LAW AND
TO ENFORCE IT WITHOUT ANY CONSIDERATION
OF CLASS, COLOR, CREED OR CONDITION.

IT IS ALSO MY DUTY TO BE OF SERVICE
TO ANYONE WHO MAY BE IN DANGER OR DISTRESS,
AND AT ALL TIMES SO CONDUCT MYSELF,
THAT THE HONOR OF THE DEPARTMENT MAY BE UPHELD.

South Plainfield, NJ

DOES YOUR LOCAL

POLICE

DEPARTMENT REPRESENT

THE COMMUNITY IT SERVES

Anthony Davila

DOES YOUR LOCAL POLICE DEPARTMENT REPRESENT THE COMMUNITY IT SERVES

Book and Cover design by Anthony Davila

First Edition: December 2017

10 9 8 7 6 5 4 3 2 1

ACKNOWLEDGEMENTS

I would like to express my thanks and appreciation to the Chiefs of Police for their time, assistance, and guidance. My gratitude also extends to the law enforcement officers and the community relations liaison officers.

Special thanks also to my law enforcement partner and friend of many years Retired Bridgeport Police Detective Harold Dimbo.

REST IN PEACE

"SONI" & "SLICK."

Notable mentions:

Jada Bush Ph.D. (ABD)

Susana Orozco, Charter Oak State College

Finally, I would like to thank my family for their motivation, support, and unwavering patience.

TABLE OF CONTENT

Dedicated to the many diverse communities in

The United States of America

Introduction

For about a year there has been much discussion across the country and around the world about police and policing in America. Social media, news media, politicians and activists have all been weighing in on this topic. Facts, supported by evidence of some sort, often get tossed to the side when the really 'hot' cases come to the frontline, and opinion and emotion wind up controlling the discussion.

One of the issues being discussed is police/community relations, the name of which is sometimes confusing to police managers and other leaders in a community. A relation or relationship is by definition a connection between persons. Some examples could be husband and wife; domestic partners; brother and sister; laborer and foreman, etc., etc. There must be at least two persons involved to have a relationship.

When discussing "the police" and "the community" there is an implied division of sorts, almost to the point of being a contradiction in purpose, and self defeating in nature. A "community" is a collective term, and is inclusive of all persons within a specific location or district, that commonly share a government, possibly a culture or ideology, maybe a history, and so on. Therefore, police are part of "the community". Where a breakdown occurs in a community is when any person or group within the community is disconnected.

Police leaders and managers often fall victim to the pitfalls of the negative aspects that are inherent in police work. Police are summoned by citizens when bad things happen. Violence is bad; car crashes are bad, crime is bad; drug abuse is bad; gangs are bad; relatives of arrestees try to make police look bad. Police expect, and are expected by citizens, to confront the bad things that occur in the community.

Surrounded by the bad in a community, police often find themselves feeling a need to separate from others in that community. Thus develops the us (the police) and them (everyone else) attitude. After the terror attacks of 9/11, police found themselves as the frontline in homeland protection, and the federal government made military equipment available to local law enforcement. The acquisition of such, and the wearing of military style fatigues for street duty, has led to the perception that the police are now over-militarized. This is a disconnect. This is what police managers and leaders must avoid. Any disconnection with the community at large is not good for the community at large! Making sure this disconnect does not occur is the major challenge of the moment. Reinventing the police image alone does not remedy disconnection, so how does the police industry accomplish non-disconnection?

The answer is simple but not easy. The answer is service. First, and always, service. Plain and simple. You've seen the predominant police motto "we serve and protect", right? Could, not a better motto be "we serve"? Isn't police protection just one part of the service that police provide, and the protection part is just... wait for it... understood?

Service to the community means involvement, commitment, and engagement with the entire community, and that includes all of the parts, including police, fire, schools, merchants, etc. Providing some law enforcement education to citizens about the total service mission of police work should be a goal for every police agency. Ensuring good service to the community means careful recruitment and personnel selection, for officers who will develop a prime focus on service first--service always. Training those carefully selected personnel on current case decisions, tactics, equipment, effective involvement in community affairs is service to the community. Having the entire police department focused on service first and service always, and engaging all members of the community in serving each other is great service for the community. Having officers use their interpersonal skills in developing and maintaining good relationships with all is a service that a community will not forget.

Changing the way one does business in a community should be purposeful. Change for the sake of change is pointless. Goal oriented change, to achieve a better level of service and professionalism, is key to developing and maintaining good community relations, not just good police relations with the community.

Public service is the function of good government. Good government is determined at the ballot box. Electing good community leaders, who in turn appoint good public servants, who believe in service first--service always, should be the primary goal of every community.

CHAPTER ONE

CURRENT DIVERSITY ISSUES WITHIN THE LAW ENFORCEMENT RANK AND FILE

The present emergency in policing has accumulated the winds of change, producing imperative discussions about what policing should look like in the 21st century. A reasonable accord is regularly difficult to accomplish given the voting demographics included, yet there is practically widespread understanding that our calling can start to turn the ship around through enhanced procuring hones. This road of change is normally surrounded inside the setting of racial and ethnic diversity, the perfect being that a police office ought to reflects the substance of the community. This is without a doubt an imperative end that can upgrade police authenticity. The call to expand the quantity of ladies in policing is less articulated, however, no less vital. Truth be told, expanding female portrayal is ostensibly a standout amongst the best approaches to decrease the rate of extra-legal force. We would be neglectful, in any case, to fix our rudder after achieving some similarity of diversity on these fronts alone.

Shockingly, the President's Task Force on 21st Century Policing received a more extensive conceptualization of diversity, opining that "Law enforcement agencies should endeavor to make a workforce that contains an expansive scope of diversity including race, sexual orientation, dialect, life encounter, and social foundation to enhance comprehension and adequacy managing all communities". This extended view is useful, yet the advantages of an assorted police compel stretch out past community engagement in ways that can propel law enforcement associations and the field of policing itself.

Each work environment has a hierarchical culture, yet the policing system is especially intense. Police initiates are introduced a culture instilled with convention, service, and solid regulating desires. It is in this condition where lukewarm perspectives rapidly merge in adjustment to the honorable aim. Our normal culture joins us in vital ways while all the while obliging our calling from headway. As the Task Force on 21st Century Policing adroitly noted, "Hierarchical culture has approach for lunch". Our resoluteness towards change is somewhat established in an absence of diversity. Advancement does not spill out of isolated resound chambers. Policing needs diversity, yet diversity of experience and thought are regularly disregarded and undervalued. Maybe it is on the grounds that these qualities are dormant, not promptly evident to the stripped eye.

The uniform that I wear is blue and the job that it speaks to is verifiably industrial. Most police officers hail from common laborers foundations and tend to lean right politically (I am blame-worthy on the two tallies). Neither one of the traits is plainly noticeable, yet both impact the route in which I see the world. My point of view has esteem, however, not the slightest bit is it superlative. Different perspectives and individual encounters are generally underrepresented or inside and out truant in policing circles. We require these voices to join our high calling.

By what method can police associations secure sound types of diversity? Educational requirements are a decent beginning stage, despite the fact that this is not really another thought. About each blue strip board gathered to ponder policing over the most recent 85 years has focused on the significance of officer instruction. Cops will talk about the relative significance of book smarts versus road smarts endlessly (to flourish, officers require both). Other than behavioral end products like higher execution and lower rates of offense, training presents information and better approaches for intuition upon the student. To profit by these advantages, police associations ought to energize officers of all positions to seek after higher learning. This can be accomplished by financing educational cost or notwithstanding boosting the limited time handle in ways that perceive the estimation of training.

It merits considering what course of study, if any, ought to be given inclination with regards to employing and advancement. The immense assortment of criminal equity examine delivered in the course of the most recent four decades has been an aid for policing and recognition with this writing is important. Be that as it may, applicants with apparently random degrees ought to be given due thought. American policing is rapidly turning into a catchall for a large group of social ills which could conceivably have a reasonable nexus to wrongdoing. In this setting even an exemplary human sciences educational programs with its accentuation on basic considering and good thinking has esteem.

Maybe what officers think about is less vital than who they examine with. At the point when police officers seek after advanced education, they regularly do as such close by a differing populace of understudies and teachers who subscribe to divergent perspectives. Presentation to the free trade of thoughts advances self-improvement and furthermore gives a remarkable chance to officers to work as accepted represetatives, speaking to their agencies and the policing calling. One of my doctoral level college teachers revealed that, were I not in his class, he would need to "imagine" me in the soul to offset classroom exchanges on law and public strategy.

Training is in no way, shape or form the main wellspring of inert diversity. Policing is regularly depicted as a calling, however, once in a while the professional call comes sometime down the road. Work understanding outside of policing or another firmly adjusted field ought not be reduced. I have military administration and security chip away at my resume, additionally put in two years educating at a non-public school for understudies with dyslexia. Hopefuls from non-customary fields have aptitudes that are out of the blue translatable. They are additionally advantaged by their capacity to draw from elective edges of reference and take part in inventive critical thinking.

Other individual encounters not generally caught on a resume likewise have esteem. Living abroad, captivating in charitable effort, and notwithstanding seeking after profound development are on the whole deep down transformative exercises. Such endeavors can encourage sympathy and mindfulness in ways that assistance us start to see over the abysses of race, class, culture, and frameworks of confidence in America.

Growing diversity in policing, latent or something else, is not a simple undertaking. There are an assortment of obstacles to overcome in the contracting procedure including homophily (the propensity to support hopefuls that take after those doing the procuring) and self-choice (applicants who seek after or maintain a strategic distance from specific callings that might be pigeonholed in different ways). Regardless of the difficulties, policing requirements to surrender its convention of self-restricting homogeneity. Identifying and creating diversity of thought and experience can reinforce the association's ability for critical thinking and take action for advancements that will lead our calling great into the 21st century.

Diversity

Now more than ever agencies are looking to fill their ranks with a diverse officer corps that reflects the populations they serve. This includes women and those from a variety of racial and ethnic backgrounds as well as other minority groups.

According to the Bureau of Justice Statistics, racial and ethnic minorities in state and local agencies made up 27 percent of full-time sworn personnel in 2013, a slight increase from 25 percent in 2007 and up from 15 percent in 1987. The number and percentage of full-time sworn female officers also increased since 1987. About 58,000 females were employed as local police officers in 2013, compared to about 27,000 in 1987. This was an increase from an estimated 5 percent to 12 percent of officers during the period. While the numbers are increasing, the profession continues to seek greater representation of women and minorities in its ranks, and many agencies are actively and aggressively recruiting these demographics. For many agencies, particularly those serving large immigrant communities, the need for racial and ethnic minorities extends far beyond traditional groups.

Furthermore, as agencies look for Officers who mirror their communities, they are also extending their definitions of diversity. From this perspective, diversity can include religion, sexual orientation, age, family background or occupation, and even neighborhood or high school.

Law enforcement requires a unique blend of traits and characteristics. Some of these include

- Empathy
- Effective communication
- Compassion
- Intelligence, and
- The ability to relate to people on a personal level.

These are traits anyone can bring to the table regardless of gender, ethnic heritage, or background. Law enforcement is a field that respects and encourages individuality. Being a member of a minority group will not limit your ability to become a law enforcement officer or your chances of career success. Law enforcement is a field where diversity matters, is encouraged, and is sought after in recruitment efforts.

Officers who speak a second language are also in high demand and in some cases are given extra compensation for their skills.

There are several groups and membership organizations devoted to the advancement of women and minorities in law enforcement. Some of these include

- National Association of Women Law Enforcement Executives
- National Center for Women & Policing
- National Association of Black Law Enforcement Executives

- Hispanic American Police Command Officers Association
- National Latino Peace Officers Association
- National Asian Peace Officers Association
- National Native American Law Enforcement Association
- American Muslim Law Enforcement Officers Association
- Gay Officers Action League

Can diverse police departments ease community tension

Police Officers armed with rifles guard the entrance to Our Lady of the Lake Hospital after a fatal shooting of police officers in Baton Rouge, Louisiana, U.S. July 17, 2016. REUTERS/Jeffrey Dubinsky

Police Officers armed with rifles guard the entrance to Our Lady of the Lake Hospital after a fatal shooting of police officers in Baton Rouge, Louisiana, U.S. July 17, 2016. REUTERS/Jeffrey Dubinsky

Normally, when the Dallas Police Department hosts its monthly testing for people interested in becoming police officers, about 70 to 80 people show up. This past weekend though, the department was expecting about 280.

The larger turnout followed a call from Dallas Police Chief David Brown to join the force after five officers were killed and others injured in a targeted ambush there last month. The chief asked young black men to stop protesting, to start applying, and to help fix the problems they see in their community.

As police-involved shootings have increased tensions between police and black communities across the country, some law enforcement agencies have put out similar calls for help in hopes of recruiting a more diverse force as one way to re-establish community trust. Leaders in Indianapolis, Minneapolis and Knoxville, Tennessee, recently refocused their efforts to attract and hire more minorities.

But officials say that having a diverse force is only one way of moving forward. In fact, they point out, research is mixed as to whether diversity helps reduce tensions. Other strategies, they say, help as much or more, such as hiring officers who know and understand the community, asking officers to build better relationships with neighborhoods they serve, reducing officers' use of aggressive arrest tactics and increasing officer training.

In Baltimore, the police force is fairly diverse — about 42 percent black, compared to 63 percent of the general population.

Yet in a scathing report released this month, the U.S. Justice Department said Baltimore's policing strategies lead to "severe and unjustified disparities in the rates of stops, searches and arrests of African Americans."

Aggressive policing tactics hardened a "long-simmering distrust of law enforcement" in parts of the community, the report said.

Conflicts between the police and the community stem from much deeper issues — ones that police are not trained to solve, said Thomas Harvey, co-founder and executive director of ArchCity Defenders, a nonprofit advocacy group that provides legal services for indigent people in Ferguson and the rest of St. Louis County, Missouri.

"Why do we as the public keep expecting police officers to fill the role of nurses, social workers, housing specialists, mental health experts, drug treatment providers, poverty experts and racial justice advocates?" he said. "We don't need more police. We need to make a commitment to address the root causes of poverty, which is at the heart of what we call crime in America."

Attempts at Diversity

Law enforcement has had some success attracting more minorities. The share of minority officers nationally has nearly doubled in three decades, growing from 14.6 to 27.3 percent since 1987, according to the U.S. Bureau of Justice Statistics.

But that still doesn't equal the share of minorities in the U.S., at 37.2 percent.

Small departments are less diverse. Departments serving less than 2,500 people are 84.4 percent white; departments that serve a million people or more are 53.4 percent white.

The Ferguson Police Department had two black officers when Michael Brown was shot and killed, two years ago, by a white police officer. To diffuse tensions, the U.S. Department of Justice recommended many changes to the police department — including hiring more minorities. Five more black officers have since been hired, including the new chief, Delrish Moss.

Yet it is unclear if having a diverse force will make a difference, Harvey said. "We can't get trapped into thinking that individual police officers can change systems."

A 2004 National Research Council report found that, "there is no credible evidence that officers of different racial or ethnic backgrounds perform differently during interactions with citizens simply because of race or ethnicity."

White officers in Cincinnati were not more likely to arrest non-white suspects, under similar circumstances, but black officers were, a 2006 study found.

Racial bias in policing comes more from the culture of police departments, said Delores Jones-Brown, founding director of the Center on Race, Crime and Justice at John Jay College of Criminal Justice in New York.

Jones-Brown said two types of training may help: one that teaches officers about their implicit biases, or stereotypes they form unconsciously, and another that teaches officers that if they are more respectful to the public, they will build community trust and justice.

The Justice Department announced in June that it would start giving its lawyers and law enforcement agents implicit bias training.

Why Minorities Don't Apply

There are two major reasons why law enforcement struggles to recruit minorities, Jones-Brown said. When police treat communities that they are all criminals, they don't want to be part of the agency. And when police enforce low-level crimes in communities of color, many people end up with criminal records that disqualify them from applying.

In Knoxville, past recruiting efforts had little success, said David Rausch, the chief of police. Of the 386 sworn officers there, 358 are white.

The lack of diversity could be the result of a lack of qualified minority candidates, Rausch said. But it also could be because of a stigma attached to police by the minority community, which has worsened with recent events across the country.

"We have folks where all they've ever heard in their life is law enforcement is the bad guys," he said. "And quite frankly, my goal in the last five years is to change that."

Last year, Knoxville police upped its efforts in recruiting minorities. As a result, Rausch estimates, about half of the applicants being interviewed are minorities, compared to the usual 20 percent.

In Indianapolis, the City-County Council voted in April to update its recruitment law to allow the chief of police to handpick 20 percent of applicants, with the rest chosen based on their qualifications, in hopes it would allow for more minority recruits.

Mirroring the Community

Sometimes the racial composition of law enforcement changes as the community changes, especially when a department tries to make the job more attractive.

That's true in Texas, where the Hispanic population has increased significantly. The share of Hispanic recruits to the Texas Highway Patrol has increased from 31 to 41 percent since 2014.

Pay has increased. So, too, has recruitment. And much of the new hiring has been in communities near the U.S.-Mexico border, said Tom Vinger, press secretary for the state's Department of Public Safety. Hispanics comprise a larger share of the population there.

Even in large police departments, only a few across the country approximately reflect the racial diversity of their communities, according to a 2015 New York Times analysis.

One of those, in Atlanta, has long been admired for its ability to attract a diverse force — 60 percent of sworn officers are black in a city where 52.4 percent of residents are.

Atlanta leaders have been deliberate about hiring minorities for decades, said Chief of Police George Turner, adding that it helps to involve minorities in recruiting. It also helps to promote minorities, he said. Twenty-three of the 43-member command staff are black, including Turner.

"If your command staff doesn't reflect your community at the top of the organization, people feel like there is a ceiling in this agency, and they don't feel like they have a chance of moving in," Turner said.

Diversity, especially in leadership, can improve problem-solving and increase innovation, said Patrick Oliver, who runs a criminal justice program at Cedarville University, in Ohio, and worked in law enforcement for 27 years.

Diversity at the top also can prevent a culture of racial bias. Managers set expectations and policies, and supervise officers, Oliver said.

Communities see diverse police departments as more legitimate and are more likely to take ownership in policing when a department is diverse, a 2000 study found.

Having a good racial mix debunks stereotypes among officers, said Tammie Hughes, and the assistant chief of police in Dallas. It also shows children in the community that "if she can be a police officer, I can be a police officer, too. Once you plant those seeds, they have something they can look forward to doing."

Not Everyone Agrees

Calling for more diversity in police departments simply distracts from the real issue, said L'lerrét Ailith, a communications manager with Black Youth Project 100, a group of 18- to 35-year-old black activists. The real issue, she said, is law enforcement is inherently anti-black and black communities do not receive enough social services.

"If the system is inherently anti-black, if the system is set up specifically to target our communities and oppress our people, regardless of what the officer looks like, regardless of what connection he has to the people he is locking up, he is still locking people up," Ailith said.

The government should defund police and invest more in health care, mental health and recreation centers, Ailith said.

Police understanding of a community may be more important than its racial composition. In Baltimore, most officers are not from the city, and three-quarters of them don't live there.

Officers who come from the community will know its history and what it needs, said Chris Burbank, a former Salt Lake City police chief who is now director of law enforcement engagement for a national nonprofit, the Center for Policing Equity.

"Whenever [a police department] is viewed as an occupying force, that is difficult for community members," Burbank said. "But when it's individuals who have grown up in the community who are now on the police force, that goes a long way."

Training also helps. In 2012, Dallas began training officers in how to ease tense situations that have the potential to spiral out of control. Hughes, the assistant chief of police, calls it teaching officers how to “slow down a bit, and approach these incidents a bit more carefully.”

Police Officer Diversity Status Impacts Their Perceptions

"Over the past few years, police involvement in the deaths of blacks in the U.S. has prompted a national debate over police tactics, training and methods. These fatal encounters have also energized the public debate about the relationship between police and blacks and other minority communities.

We and others have explored public views about the police, race and the use of force. This project helps to fill an important knowledge gap: What do police think about these recent events, and what do they see as the key issues and concerns facing them and their profession? And how do the views of police officers compare with those of the public? To the best of my knowledge, this is among the largest and certainly the most wide-ranging survey of police officers ever attempted."

The study itself provides overall statistics on a great many subjects and also breaks those statistics down based upon the race or ethnicity of the officer, their gender, size of the police department, length of time on the force, and rank. With regard to certain topics, they also included the statistics with regard to the general public.

The subjects covered include the following:

- The motivations behind protests/demonstrations
- Officer satisfaction with their Department
- How strongly committed they are to making their agency successful
- The fairness of the disciplinary procedures
- Whether they feel respected by the general public
- Whether they trust the general public
- Pride in their work
- Job frustration
- Whether their job makes them angry
- Whether the job made them more callous
- Whether the residents of the areas they patrol share their values and beliefs
- Whether an aggressive rather than courteous approach is more effective in certain neighborhoods
- Whether some people can only be brought to reason the hard, physical way
- The police department's relationship with whites
- The police department's relationship with Hispanics
- The police department's relationship with Asians
- Whether the country has made the changes needed to assure equal rights for blacks
- Whether the deaths of blacks at the hands of police are isolated incidents
- Whether they favor a ban on assault-style weapons
- Whether they favor the use of body cameras

- Whether they believe the country's marijuana laws should be relaxed
- Whether they support legalizing marijuana for both private and medical use
- Whether they see themselves as just protectors or as enforcers
- Serious concerns about their physical safety at least sometimes when they are on the job
- Frequency of physical struggles or fights with suspects who were resisting arrest
- How well the general public understands the risks and challenges they face
- How they would handle a situation in which doing what is morally right requires breaking department rules
- Praise of their departmental leadership
- Concerns regarding resource limitations
- Ratings for training and equipping officers to do their jobs
- Ratings of use-of-force policies and training
- Striking the right balance between acting decisively versus taking time to assess a situation
- Departmental treatment of white versus officers who are members of minority groups
- Whether officers should be required to intervene when they believe another officer is about to use unnecessary force
- Whether their department has taken action to improve relations with black residents

A few key findings from the study were as follows:

Most police officers feel respected by the public and, in turn, believe officers have little reason to distrust most people.

Large majorities of white, black and Hispanic officers agree that police and whites in their communities get along. But striking differences emerge when the focus shifts to police relations with racial and ethnic minorities. A consistently smaller share of black officers than their white or Hispanic colleagues say the police have a positive relationship with minorities in the community they serve. Roughly a third of all black officers (32%) characterize relations with blacks in their community as either excellent or good, while majorities of white and Hispanic officers (60% for both) offer a positive assessment.

At the same time, only about half of all black officers (46%) but large majorities of Hispanic (71%) and white (76%) officers say relations between police and Hispanics are excellent or good. Similarly, three-quarters of all black officers but 91% of white officers and 88% of Hispanic Officers rate relations with Asians in their communities positively.

Most officers agree that in order to be effective, police need to understand the people in the neighborhoods they patrol.

Yet the degree to which officers value local knowledge varies significantly by the officer's race and gender. Fully 84% of black officers and 78% of Hispanics say knowledge of the people, places and culture of the neighborhoods they patrol is very important to be effective at their job, a view shared by 69% of whites. Female

Officers also are more likely than males to place a premium on local knowledge (80% vs. 71%).

Seven-in-ten (72%) say that poorly performing officers are not held accountable.

And when the topic turns more broadly to the state of race relations, virtually all white officers (92%) but only 29% of their black colleagues say that the country has made the changes needed to assure equal rights for blacks. Not only do the views of white officers differ from those of their black colleagues, but they stand far apart from those of whites overall: 57% of all white adults say no more changes are needed, as measured in the Center's survey of the general public.

Relatively few officers (22%) say their job often makes them feel angry, but a significant share (49%) say it sometimes makes them feel this way. Officers who say their job often makes them feel angry seem to be less connected to the citizens they serve. Fully 45% say very few or none of the people in the neighborhoods they serve share their values. Only 20% of officers who say they hardly ever or never feel angry say the same.

Officers in larger departments are less likely than those in smaller departments to say they share values with the people in the areas where they patrol.

White officers are significantly more likely than black officers to associate negative emotions with their job.

White male officers were more likely to have physically struggled or fought with a suspect who was resisting arrest in the past month.

Blacks and department administrators (59%) are the only two major groups in which a majority is more concerned that officers will act too quickly than worry that they will wait too long before responding to a situation.

Among black officers, 69% say the protests were sincere efforts to force police accountability – more than double the proportion of whites (27%) who share this view. Female officers, older police and department administrators also are more likely than male officers, younger police and rank-and-file officers to believe protesters genuinely seek police accountability.

A narrow majority of officers (56%) feel that in some neighborhoods being aggressive is more effective than being courteous, while 44% agree or strongly agree that hard, physical tactics are necessary to deal with some people.

On both measures, a larger share of younger, less senior officers and those with less than five years of experience favor these techniques, while proportionally fewer older, more experienced officers or department administrators endorse them.

Younger officers and white Officers are more likely than older or black officers to say they have become more callous.

Officers who report they have grown more callous are also more likely than their colleagues to endorse aggressive or physically harsh tactics with some people or in some parts of the community. They also are more likely than other officers to say they are frequently angered or frustrated by their jobs or to have been involved in a physical or verbal confrontation with a citizen in the past month or to have fired their service weapon while on duty at some point in their careers.

It is difficult to discern with these data whether increased callousness is a primary cause or a consequence of feelings of anger or frustration, or attitudes toward aggressive tactics. However, the data suggest that these feelings and behaviors are related. For example, officers who sense they have become more callous on the job are about twice as likely as those who say they have not to say their job nearly always or often makes them feel angry (30% vs. 12%). They also are more likely to feel frustrated by their job (63% vs. 37%).

Among those officers who say they have become more callous, about four-in-ten (38%) physically struggled or fought with a suspect in the previous month compared with 26% of those who say they have not become more insensitive.

About half of black officers (53%) say that whites are treated better than minorities in their department or agency when it comes to assignments and promotions. Few Hispanic (19%) or white officers (1%) agree. About six-in-ten white and Hispanic officers say minorities and whites are treated the same (compared with 39% of black officers).

Among white officers, 31% say they have discharged their service firearm while on duty. A smaller share of black (21%) and Hispanic (20%) officers report doing the same.

Suffice it to say that this study confirms what social science researcher Brene' Brown has been saying with regard to empathy, some of which is as follows:

Empathy is a skill set, the core of which is perspective taking

Perspective taking is normally taught or modeled by parents. The more your perspective is in line with the dominant culture, the less you were probably taught about perspective taking. In the United States, the majority culture is white, Judeo-Christian, middle class, educated, and straight.

We all see the world in a different way, based upon our information, insight and experiences. Among other things, this takes into account our age, sexual orientation, physical ability, gender, race, ethnicity, and spirituality.

We can't take off the lens from which we see the world. Perspective taking is listening to the truth as other people experience it and acknowledging it as the truth. What you see is as true, real and honest as what I see, so let me be quite for a minute, listen and learn about what you see. Let me get curious about what you see. Let me ask questions about what you see.

Empathy is incompatible with shame and judgment. Staying out of judgment requires understanding.

"Empathy can be a transformative tool for deconstructing unconscious biases and building understanding between people of different backgrounds."

What does diversity within the police force have to do in that regard? "Integration and assimilation are very positive things because they enable people to see other perspectives, which is the core of empathy." Furthermore, "empathy is an amazing form of bias reduction and in keeping your biases in check."

However, from all appearances, the diversity within the police force is not promoting the empathy it could because otherwise, the differences in perceptions based upon race, ethnicity, gender and other such things wouldn't be quite so glaring. Police departments might want to do more to benefit from such diversity.

Furthermore, the results of this study confirm the need for police departments to develop a collaborative relationship with their community, among other things. I published an article on this subject on Oct. 29, 2015 which was republished by American Police Beat Magazine, which claims to be "The Voice of the Nation's Law Enforcement Community. Largest, most widely-read and respected publication for Law Enforcement in the U.S."

As mentioned in The Connection Between Empathy Toward Others and Ethics, "Empathy toward 'others' is strongly associated with ethics." As referenced in that article, the less "empathy" one has for "others," the easier it is for them to commit bad acts toward such "others" and to rationalize the morality of their behavior.

Along those lines, it bears mentioning that the study stated as follows with regard to moral dilemmas:

"The situations police face on the job can often present moral dilemmas. When asked how they would advise a fellow officer in an instance where doing what is morally the right thing would require breaking a department rule, a majority of police (57%) say they would advise their colleague to do the morally right thing.

Four-in-ten say they would advise the colleague to follow the department rule. There's a significant racial divide on this question: 63% of white officers say they would advise doing the morally right thing, even if it meant breaking a department rule; only 43% of black officers say they would give the same advice."

However, "moral judgments are true or false only relative to some particular standpoint (for instance, that of a culture or a historical period) and that no standpoint is uniquely privileged over all others.... [Therefore], we should refrain from passing moral judgments on beliefs and practices characteristic of cultures other than our own."

As Gary Saul Morson said, "empathy is not all of morality, but it is where it begins."

This is further explained by author Robert Wright in his TED Talk Progress is not a zero-sum game, wherein he said the following: "We need a major round of moral progress in the world–see less hatred among groups, less bigotry–racial groups, religious groups, whatever. There is no alternative.

Moral progress–morality is based upon self-interest–when your welfare is correlated with mine. That set the moral progress so far. It is in everyone's self-interest to further the moral evolution.

Why do so many people around the world hate us? To really understand why someone in a very different culture does something is a morally redeeming accomplishment. True understanding is an expansion of your moral compass."

As Tim Leberecht so eloquently said, "Empathy, the experience of understanding another person's condition from their perspective, is the link between ourselves and 'the other' and as such is a critical concept for any functioning peaceful human society. It serves as the prerequisite of moral imagination and judgment; only if we are capable of accepting the other as a being with feelings do we feel compelled to act morally."

Moreover, the study indicated that white male officers felt that the disciplinary process and opportunities for promotion were more fair than did other groups. As such, those officers who fall outside of the dominant culture might be more inclined to follow the departmental rules.

We may all perceive things as we wish. However, the facts are the facts.

In 2010 alone, the costs associated with civil judgments and settlements related to police misconduct were $346,512,800, according to the CATO Institute.

As Richard Emery and Ilann Margalit Maazel said in their article titled Why Civil Rights Lawsuits Do Not Deter Police Misconduct: The Conundrum of Indemnification and a Proposed Solution, "In thousands of cases around the country, civil rights plaintiffs successfully sue police officers for violating the Constitution. Yet, day in and day out, police officers make arrests without probable cause, use excessive force, deny arrestees medical treatment, and otherwise violate the Constitution with near impunity. Why don't civil lawsuits deter this reprehensible conduct? The answer, this essay posits, lies in the conundrum of indemnification. [Cities regularly indemnify] police officers regardless of whether they acted intentionally, recklessly, or brutally; whether or not they violated federal or state law; or whether or not they violated the rules and regulations of the Police Department."

As it stands now, the tax payers are paying the salaries of those whose actions lead to such tragic results and then they flip the bill for the financial consequences that ensue. Furthermore, there's not only no liability on the part of the offending parties, but they also seem to keep their jobs, perks, and all.

If this doesn't provide some proof to support Robert Wright's position that "It is in everyone’s self-interest to further the moral evolution," I don't know what will.

All things being equal, many police officers who are members of the dominant culture could use a good dose of empathy toward "others," and the same could be said of many members of the dominant culture who don't happen to be police officers.

CHAPTER TWO

LAW ENFORCEMENT COMMUNITY RELATION EFFORTS

We can easily notice nowadays how diverse the UK is becoming. It is highly evident, especially in the more urban areas of the country. The police equality and diversity policy and attitude is, by necessity, changing and adapting to mirror the demographics of the communities in which they serve.

The police constantly strives to ensure a very strong, even unbreakable, link between the police force and members of the community. This has to take race and ethnic issues into consideration. The police force must therefore negate all suggestions of discrimination, however slight, and ensure that the modern police force in England and Wales is fair on everyone.

Apart from being a more ethical stance to take, the level of police equality and diversity will have a large impact upon the service that the force is able to provide to our many communities. By becoming more diverse, the police force is able to integrate itself into our communities much better than it ever has before. By constructing itself from officers of other ethnicities, the police force can be far more approachable to those of a different race, origin, gender or sexuality. The public can therefore feel more inclined to working with the police to promote a greater standard of living and quality of life.

Building bridges is all part of crime prevention. By treating all members of the community with dignity and respect, the police force will enable itself to gain a greater understanding and create a strong yet trustworthy presence. The co-operation of members of any community can greatly help in the reduction of crime. Tensions between the police and the public will thus be eased and a more relaxed, yet effective, atmosphere can be established.

To gain the most from police officers regarding police equality and diversity, the forces across England and Wales are taking several measures. Some forces ask officers to register their own languages, experiences with other cultures and unusual skills so gain from their experience. Other police forces have given aid to female members of the force to help them with their children. In Wales, it is increasingly common to see the police force employ gay officers in order to reduce tension between the police force and the homosexual communities.

The police also operate a scheme of encouraging those of an ethnic minority to join the force. There are currently not enough applicants from such groups and thus the police force has to encourage a greater participation from such communities. This is helping to improve the quality and diversity of the service provided by the police in England and Wales.

Police equality and diversity is paving the way for a far more public-friendly and effective law enforcement service in England and Wales. In doing so the public will be more aware of police activities and all communities will feel more able to work with the police to improve the quality of life in our local residencies. Being diverse is simply what makes the police so able and capable in its crime fighting mission

The Diversity Relation Bureau is dedicated to addressing various needs within our multicultural community by supporting community initiatives, promoting inclusivity, implementing outreach programs, developing relationships by engaging community members, providing educational training, mediating in times of crisis and conducting reviews of all hate/bias motivated crimes and incidents.

Community Engagement

The Diversity Relations Bureau liaises with community-based agencies, educational facilities, government, law enforcement agencies, and members of the community to develop and maintain strong relationships and facilitate mutual understanding and trust. This is achieved through the sharing of information, open communication and dialogue that promotes education of cultures, religions and current events that affect our community.

Crisis Intervention

Monitor local and global events that have the potential to impact our community. Intervene at the community level through our stakeholder and advisory committees to implement awareness through initiatives. This is done through collaborative partnerships with community-based agencies and organizations.

Education and Training

In collaboration with community partners and government agencies, develop training and seminars for all police personnel to ensure they possess the necessary knowledge and skills to provide fair and equitable service to the various communities within our jurisdiction. Identify and deliver programs that address cultural awareness and promote inclusivity throughout the Region of Peel.

Hate Crime

The Diversity Relations Bureau reviews and monitors all hate/bias motivated reports to ensure compliance with departmental policies. Provide assistance to investigative personnel in relation to hate/bias motivated incidents and crimes. Track trends and patterns and in conjunction with community partners ensure a greater awareness of hate crime and incidents. Prepare an annual report for Statistics Canada on hate crime in our jurisdiction.

Media Outreach

Through both social and mainstream media the Diversity Relations Bureau endeavours to provide cultural awareness through community engagement and outreach, police initiatives and campaigns, and through collaborative community events.

- Diversity Relations Bureau is responsible the following:
- Develop and maintain polices related to diversity issues to enhance our police service's ability to better serve the community
- Monitor police occurrence reports to ensure officers comply with said policies
- Provide assistance/guidance with any diversity related investigations when required
- Develop, deliver and amend, when required, all in-service awareness education modules relating to diversity and/or hate crime issues
- Conflict mediation for inter-community and/or police-community concerns

- Extensive community outreach initiatives to ensure the needs of the various communities within our policing jurisdiction are identified and addressed
- Develop and maintain partnerships with all communities to ensure police-community interactions are non-offensive without compromising officer safety practices
- Develop and maintain partnerships with other service providers within our policing jurisdiction (i.e.: community-based ethno-specific agencies, school boards, media, government)
- Identify, develop and maintain a networking partnership with other diversity focused service providers to strengthen our policies and practices and to share or seek out "Best Practices"

Successes:

The Peel Regional Police routinely reviews existing policies and practices to ensure we maintain a high level of service delivery. As an organization we are proud of our achievements in addressing the needs of our culturally diverse region and have been recognized for some of our initiatives.

The Peel Regional Police was the first police service to develop and issue all members with a handbook on diversity. This text, Police, Race and Ethnicity is now in its third edition and is issued to many other police services as well as utilized as a training aid by many law enforcement agencies

The initiatives undertaken by the Peel Regional Police to improve race relations, have been recognized by several community based agencies:

- The Chinese Businessmen's Association
- The National Indo-Canadian Association
- Peel Multicultural Council
- Carrassauga and Carabram Planning Committees
- Multicultural Inter-Agency Group of Peel

The Peel Regional Police has had input into the provincial standardize police training on diversity issues and representatives have delivered its Diversity Awareness module to law and criminology students at the Secondary School, community college and university level. We have also assisted community-based agencies develop training modules and policies.

We have successfully partnered with community based, ethno-specific agencies when patterns of recurring law enforcement problems have been identified. Through these partnerships, we have been able to reduce the recidivism rate with certain offences, making the overall community safer.

By establishing partnerships with the communities within our policing jurisdiction, recruiting initiatives to attract a broader representation of the region's population have proved successful.

These same initiatives have been applied internally to ensure the ranks reflect our community.

The Peel Regional Police work with several community advisory committees to ensure our community's needs are properly identified and addressed in our service delivery.

Representatives from our specialized units, serve as advisors on Boards of several community based agencies. Members also participate on planning and support committees throughout the region.

The Peel Regional Police Diversity Relations Bureau officers have been actively involved in the planning of an international Conference for Hate Crime as well as involved in the planning and delivery of several smaller, locally held Diversity Issues/Hate Crime workshops.

How to improve community-police relations? Here are two approaches.

Neighborhood Police Officer Baron Coleman works to build trust between the police and Detroit residents

- Trust between police and the black community has taken a major hit after the spate of recent police shootings of black men around the country. So this week, we're taking a look at how some Michigan cities are trying to rebuild that trust, starting at the neighborhood level.

Its 10:30 a.m. and Officer Baron Coleman's cell phone is already blowing up with voice mail messages from Detroit residents. One guy calls about a possible squatter in the neighborhood, an older lady calls to report some drug activity at the BP gas station on 7 Mile Road, another woman leaves a message about how cars are being stripped and dumped in a lot by her house.

Coleman is what's called a Neighborhood Police Officer, one of roughly 35 in the city. His beat is all the neighborhood's in the 8th precinct on Detroit's west side. Theoretically every person who lives in that precinct has Officer Coleman's cell phone number, though on a recent patrol last week, only one out of the six residents he spoke to knew who he was; none had his number. He made sure to give his business card with his cell phone number on it to each person.

The whole point of the neighborhood police program, which started in Detroit three years ago, is to build trust between cops and residents. Right now, he says, there's a "disconnect" between the police and communities of color - not just in Detroit but across the country. It's his job to be "the connect" between the two groups and build trust where there often isn't any.

"When you call 911, officers are coming to an emergency," he explains. "They get in, catch the bad guy and go. But with a neighborhood police officer, they might call me about anything from a barking dog, to a basketball rim in the street, not liking the neighbor, neighbor not liking them, people parking on their grass.

It's like that commercial that used to come on years ago, father and son, no job too big, no job too small. We're the neighborhood police officers, we fix it all."

Coleman's the first one to tell you: he understand why people -- specifically African Americans -- don't trust the police. Much of the time, he says, the only interaction blacks have with police is when there's a conflict or criminal activity; the majority of their interactions with police are negative.

Coleman often helps out with block clubs and cookouts, so his trunk is filled with oven mitts, camping chairs and juice boxes.

- But "if I come by your street every day, wave at you, be nice to you, be nice to your family..." trust will start to develop. That philosophy helps explains all the stuff he has in the trunk of his cop car: oven mitts (so he can man the grill at neighborhood cookouts), bright red camping chairs (so he can hang out at the park if there's a game or party), and a crate of juice boxes (for the kids in the neighborhood).

As the neighborhood police officer, Coleman's also responsible for staying in touch with the businesses in the area: gas stations, liquor stores, Coney Islands, and barbershops, often checking in on them once or twice a week to make sure things are going smoothly.

But does it cut down on crime?

Rob Chapman is with the U.S. Department of Justice's Office of Community Oriented Policing Services (COPS). He says it's "very difficult" to measure whether or not community policing efforts like Detroit's neighborhood police program cut down on crime, but there are studies that show how similar efforts improve residents' satisfaction with police services. "It increases the trust in their law enforcement agency and it decreases fear of crime," says Chapman.

At its core, Chapman says community policing is good policing. "It's going out and forming relationships, enhancing relationships, institutionalizing them so that when a crisis happens you can rely on trust and goodwill, not scrambling to build relationships."

The Huffington Post has this summary of how federal funding for COPS has ebbed and flowed depending on who's in the White House:

By the 1990s, the philosophy of community policing had become widely known in law enforcement. DOJ's Community Oriented Policing Services office was formed in 1994 as part of President Bill Clinton's sweeping crime package. Created to support local agencies' community policing efforts, COPS sought to get 100,000 officers hired and distribute billions in grants. COPS Principal Deputy Director Sandra Webb told HuffPost that the office has provided community policing funding for about 70 percent of law enforcement agencies nationwide.

But while community policing can and does occur without federal support, Webb explained that attention for COPS' efforts waned after Clinton's initial investment, and the department's budget declined significantly, from a high of $1.6 billion in 1998 to just $208 million for 2015. (In 2009, $550 million was budgeted, but the stimulus package also allocated a separate one-time $1 billion for hiring officers). The George W. Bush administration actually proposed completely eliminating the COPS program in all eight of its annual budget proposals, though it was never successful in accomplishing that.

Chapman says the COPS program doled out $134.5 million last year, and President Barack Obama's Task Force on 21st Century Policing calls for a renewed focus on community policing.

Here comes the middle man

In Washtenaw County, instead of sending out police to the neighborhoods to build trust, they send out a middle man, like 37-year old Terrence Benjamin Samuel, Jr. He grew up on the streets of Ypsilanti and has served time in state and federal prison. "I did what every gangster could do but die: drugs, gangs, robberies ... everything."

Building Police-Community Relationships

The relationship of the police to the community should be harmonious. The community relies upon the police department to "protect and serve" and the police, in return, rely upon community support and cooperation in order to be effective. When communication and trust deteriorate, tensions build between the community and police and undermine their shared goal of safer communities.

Poor communication between the police and communities served was the problem listed most frequently, in a variety of ways, by police and community members surveyed. When asked what the main problems are when it comes to police-community relations, police leaders listed "language barriers," "connecting with the community," and "lack of meaningful communication on both sides and lack of understanding of police practices" as obstacles to better relations. This list is similar to the one provided by community members, who listed "lack of communication," "language barriers," and "lack of relationships" as barriers to getting along with the police.

Communication is an active, not passive, process. It is not merely the provision of information or demands to another, rather it is a process of engagement, of listening, of seeking out and understanding what the other is trying to express. Where communities and police departments are communicating successfully with each other, how are they doing it? What are specific cities doing, either successfully or not so successfully? Are formal communications plans (at least between police leaders and the community) the way to go? What process should be instituted that would allow one group to understand the other so that trust might flourish?

In this section, we will discuss strategies that police can use in reaching out to communities. Such strategies include: incorporating accountability and transparency; creating opportunities for educational exchanges such as "citizens' police academies;" establishing regular neighborhood meetings and maintaining communication and follow-up between these meetings; and organizing forums to discuss policies, tactics, or technology of interest to community. We will also examine the strategies used by the communities to reach out to and educate the police about the community, such as maintaining communication and follow up between neighborhood meetings, canvassing for volunteers and establishing an active roster, and raising awareness of neighborhood meetings.

What the Police Should Do

It is necessary to incorporate accountability and transparency

The police are responsible for trying to make communities safe by working to prevent criminal acts and enforcing the law. They are accountable to the community and its assessment of police successes and failures in preventing, fighting, and solving crimes. The police must also be open and transparent when dealing with the community and describing crime-fighting efforts.

This mantle of responsibility for fighting crime carries with it the obligation for the police to respect the rights of the community members, since the police can only accomplish their task with the cooperation and support of the community. When police fail to respect the rights of residents and police and political leaders fail to hold those who engage in misconduct accountable, the police-community relationship is put in jeopardy.

In our interviews, many members of the community noted the lack of trust in the police, due in large part to a perceived, or real, lack of accountability and transparency by the police. One area where there is a great deal of concern about accountability is in the handling of misconduct complaints. Police leaders must describe to the public how police are held accountable for misconduct. In addition to describing the investigative and disciplinary procedures, the police need to show outcomes that assure the public that those who do not follow the department's rules, or the law, are disciplined appropriately.

In efforts to educate the public about policing, accountability systems should be described fully. Obvious questions from the public include:

- How does the internal investigation work?
- What are possible outcomes of an internal investigation?
- Who decides about any disciplinary action, if misconduct is found?

- Are there external oversight mechanisms? How do they work?
- How long will all of the investigations typically take?
- What is required of a complainant in this process?
- What does the FBI or District Attorney's office do, in relation to misconduct investigations or criminal prosecutors of law enforcement officials?

Community members want to be heard when they voice concerns about police actions and they want to understand what to expect. Residents also want police leaders to be candid and forthcoming. By educating the community about accountability systems and being as transparent as possible in general, but especially when it comes to community concerns about specific issues or incidents, police leaders will help lay the foundation for building trust.

The community wants more out of "community policing" than just to be an extra set of eyes and ears for the police. The community wants to have input into how the neighborhood is governed and policed. Although there is evidence from our surveys that the police departments are actively reaching out to the community the police are still hesitant to include the community in decision making or sharing power. Both of these elements are necessary if the community is to be a true partner with the police in making neighborhoods safer. The community should be allowed input into police officer evaluations and reviewing complaints. The community should be allowed input into police officer promotions and, as noted earlier, promotions should be based on the officers' community policing efforts and involvement with the community (both on and off duty) as well as other merits.

In addition to community meetings and forums another method of for the police to discern concerns of the community is through surveys. A common method of conducting surveys is through mailing them out but, as described by Maya Harris West in her book, Community-centered Policing: A Force for Change, the Lincoln Police Department (Nebraska) uses police recruits to make random telephone calls throughout the year to those members of the community based upon three difference police-citizen contacts: drivers in accidents; victims of crime; and those who received a ticket.

The use of the police recruits allows them first hand exposure to community concerns and input. For the Lincoln Police Department, the surveys provide insight into the perception of its police practices by the community. For example, through the surveys, it was revealed that there was dissatisfaction with the lack of police follow up on crimes reported by the victims. Upon investigation, the department discovered that it was not a lack of follow up but rather a lack of communicating to those victims that there was no follow up possible/necessary in their particular case. As a result, officers investigating these calls were instructed to explain to the victim whether follow up was possible or not and why, so the victim would know what to expect.

Create opportunities for educational exchanges between the police and the community.

A common method of educational exchange is for police departments to host a "citizens' police academy" to offer members of the community a chance to experience and better understand aspects of the police officer's job. citizens police academies, which utilize a one-way educational process consisting of police instructing the community, should be supplemented by departmental consultation with residents as its policies and strategies are developed.

Create "citizens police academies" to educate the community about policing.

Citizen academies are becoming very common and are popular with the public because the creation of citizens' police academies by police departments allows community members some insight into police policies, tactics and training and is seen as a positive development by the community. In order to provide a better view of policing and the obstacles which police officers face a police chief suggests the "use of citizen police academies and scenarios for civilians to illustrate what officers face on the job."

The citizens' police academy typically runs one night a week for approximately two to three hours over a period of 9 to 16 weeks. Police personnel typically teach the classes, with trainers with specific expertise responsible for certain sessions. Topics covered include:

- Crime-scene investigation
- Traffic accident investigation
- Drug investigations
- Criminal law
- Patrol procedures
- Communications
- Crime prevention
- Courtroom procedures

The citizens' academies also offer the opportunity for members of communities to see "behind the scenes" work of the police departments, with presentations on subjects including: anti-gang, SWAT, and bomb squads; narcotics and vice investigations; and traffic radar enforcement.

The training is not all lectures -- citizens' academies offer members of the community opportunities for hands-on training on firearms, fingerprinting, precision-course driving, defensive tactics, criminal investigations, mock traffic stops, and crime scene processing. There may also be field trips or tours to police-related facilities, including detention centers, emergency communications center, crime labs, special investigative units, and ride-alongs with officers during a working shift.

Because of the popularity of the academies, one police chief wants to expand the citizen's academy, as well as create a "mini-academy" which is focused on more particular issues such as gangs or drugs (for particular neighborhoods). Another police department, in addition to a 13-week (one day a week) police academy program, has created a "Senior Citizens Police Academy" which runs over the course of one week, four hours a day, and a "Teen Police Academy" which is scheduled during the summer for a week.

Establish regular neighborhood meetings between the police and community members.

A regularly scheduled weekly or monthly meeting with the community liaison officer, as well as area patrol officers, allows the community time to voice their concerns and get to know the officers (and the officers to know the members of the community). The meetings are important in that they help engage the community in a meaningful way, identify and prioritize issues of concern, monitor changing community needs, and help solve problems before they grow. The regular meetings offer an opportunity to discover "what is going on in the neighborhood and offer a great conduit for [communication] and there is lots of input from various people" according to one chief of police while another states that the meetings offer "open communication, partnerships and collaboration."

Maintain communication and follow-up between meetings.

The neighborhood meetings provide an opportunity for the police and the community to interact. Beyond meetings, there need to be open lines of communication so that community members feel comfortable approaching the police with non-emergency concerns. This is especially important in communities where some members may not feel at ease to raise issues of concern publicly at regularly scheduled, formal meetings.

Other communication techniques include:

i. community fulfillment studies.

ii. recordings, data and preparing made unreservedly accessible for credit.

iii. web with web throws, intuitive sites, web conferencing.

iv. gatherings (huge and little), for both the community pioneers and also individuals in the city and watch officers.

v. ensuring materials are accessible in the dialects of the groups served.

vi. Compose gatherings to talk about arrangements, strategies, or innovation important to the community.

Arrangements, strategies, and innovation utilized by police officers might be a secret to most individuals from the community. At the point when concerns are raised about specific arrangements, strategies, or innovation – or when police pioneers ought to sensibly anticipate that worries will be raised – community discussions ought to be composed to give data to inhabitants.

The gatherings ought to likewise be utilized to give the chance to community individuals to pass on related concerns.

For instance, if a police office is thinking about giving Tasers to use by its officers, police pioneers ought to counsel with the community and portray why they are thinking about utilizing the innovation. Police pioneers ought to get input from the community and react to its worries. In any event, if a division has chosen to buy another weapon and has neglected to counsel with the community, it ought to sort out a gathering to show how and why the weapon is utilized, why the office picked it, how the officers will be prepared on it, et cetera. Worries in regards to specific strategies, strategies, and innovation can be extraordinarily lessened if police set aside the opportunity to counsel with, and instruct, general society about its choices.

Solicit for volunteers and set up a dynamic program.

One of the huge difficulties confronting community police relations is to keep up the proceeding with intrigue and cooperation of individuals from the community in neighborhood boards. The police division has congruity on the grounds that, as an office, it will guarantee that it will constantly have an officer appointed to liaise with the area (a paid position) rather than the community individuals are for the most part volunteers who need to confer their extra time and assets to the gatherings. As one community part takes note of "The economy is intense, individuals simply don't have room schedule-wise to put the exertion into going to standard gatherings so gatherings are normally gone to by more seasoned individuals." Working at least one employments, family responsibilities and different weights may show impediments to some for a long haul duty. There are likewise different difficulties in campaigning for volunteers. In talking about the difficulties experienced in attempting to enroll people from littler minority gatherings, one community part disclosed to us that individuals from the littler gatherings "seem more detached or reluctant to advocate, it is difficult to identify the pioneers or regardless of the possibility that there is one".

Another issue is the community's opposition toward the police in few neighborhoods, particularly in bringing down salary ranges or in neighborhoods where occupants have persevered what they consider racially-one-sided policing or experienced "rougher" policing strategies in connection to issues like drug managing or posse brutality. That enmity may likewise manifest itself towards those people or gatherings who are believed to "collaborate" with the police in such program as Block Watch or neighborhood boards of trustees and consequently make volunteers less ready to approach.

Bring issues to light of neighborhood gatherings.

The time, area, and date of police-community gatherings should be announced on a consistent and proactive premise. One community dissident uses "radio, occasions and celebrations, informal, ESL and education programs" to select community individuals and bring issues to light, while another states that to connect, he utilizes "mailings to those outside the system, religious, business, minorities: for instance for the Burmese community, a volunteer will interpret [the material] and liaise with that community".

Identify and use community resources.

For creating assets and mastery, an area can utilize "asset mapping" or "resource mapping" which is a procedure of peddling the community of the assets which dwell inside it, budgetary, specialized and individual ability, in order to utilize them in the most effective way. This can be expert through way to-entryway overviews or through forums. Plainly one of the assets is the police officers in the area, yet there are likewise the social administration agencies, the nearby schools, neighborhood organizations and legislative agencies, all of which may have programs accessible (or a longing to take an interest in programs) to address community concerns if drew closer. While not an end in itself, building up a stock of community resources is likewise a vehicle for bringing individuals from the community together, to meet, and to gain from each other. Asset mapping will help with instating exchange with the police and the community about what assets are accessible, what can be accomplished and the dedication required.

CHAPTER THREE

LAW ENFORCEMENT'S BLUE LINE NOT AS UNITED AS ONE MAY THINK

As of late, law enforcement all through the nation watched National Police Week to respect kindred officers who have kicked the bucket in the line of obligation.

One officer regarded was Montrell Jackson, the Baton Rouge police officer who was murdered not as much as seven days after the police-included shooting of Alton Sterling. Days before his awkward demise, Officer Jackson depicted on Facebook his remarkable battles as a black police officer. He related the terrible looks he got: from groups that did not believe him when he was in uniform, and from different officers that thought of him as a danger when he was in casually dressed.

His experience sensationalizes the requirement for a Police Week that spotlights not just on the officers who have been lost, additionally on the progressions that will enhance community-police trust, and also officer and open security.

Shockingly, Congress has spent for the previous week considering repetitive enactment that will just augment the crevice amongst groups and law enforcement, with no additional security advantage. These bills, the Thin Blue Line Act and the Probation Officer Protection Act of 2017, which are planned for a vote in the House, organize troublesome political pandering over important change.

The Thin Blue Line Act adjusts the government criminal code to make executing or focusing on law enforcement, firefighters, or people on call an irritating variable in deciding if a capital punishment is justified. This bill is misinformed and unnecessarily duplicative. Government law as of now stipulates that wrongdoings carried out against law enforcement can be viewed as an exasperating element in measuring the burden of the death penalty, and each of the 50 states have laws set up that uplift sentences for violations against law enforcement.

The Probation Officer Protection Act would permit government post trial agents to lead warrantless captures of any individual an officer claims is blocking their work, well past their present expert to capture just those abusing a state of their discharge. This hazardous enactment raises genuine Fourth Amendment concerns and, if sanctioned, will prompt an expansion in tense physical experiences that post trial agents are badly prepared to deal with.

As opposed to advancing these ineffective measures, the NAACP Legal Defense and Educational Fund, Inc. (LDF) supports individuals from Congress and people the nation over to find out about and work to execute a portion of the changes that will change policing to the regale of all.

Genuine change must begin with preparing. Hostile to predisposition preparing, for instance, instructs law enforcement officers about the express and verifiable inclinations that can represent their basic leadership. By confronting inclinations head-on, officers can significantly decrease racial differences in the criminal equity framework.

There's likewise utilization of-compel preparing, which shows officers precisely when and how different sorts of drive ought to be utilized, and de-heightening preparing, which can assist keep officers from falling back on constrain in any case.

While this may appear to be instinctive, enlists for the most part burn through seven times a bigger number of hours figuring out how to shoot a firearm than they do figuring out how to defuse a circumstance. If police divisions all through the nation were ordered to give these courses, and given government financing to do as such, officers would be much better prepared to carry out their employments securely and unavoidably.

Better preparing must be combined with better information. We urgently require exhaustive enactment that makes government subsidizing to nearby offices dependent upon unrivaled information accumulation and revealing, with the goal that we can better identify beset police offices and execute supportable arrangements. Unless we comprehend the extent of the issue, we can't want to understand it.

These are only a couple of the means that, when joined with substantive responsibility instruments, including, for instance, restricting government supports just to police divisions that actualize sacred policing hones, could convey enduring change to communities over the United States.

Founding and systematizing these genuinely necessary changes could barely be more dire. Regarding the sacrifice of fallen police officers ought not keep Congress from standing up to the way that our country's policing troubles are not around a couple of rotten ones or an absence of 'law and request.' The passings of African-Americans on account of police are not separated occurrences, and they will keep on tearing at the texture of our country until the point that we address the underlying drivers.

Congress must be a piece of the arrangement. Change regularly begins at the neighborhood level, yet it can be energized and quickened by shrewdly made enactment. Tragically, charges like the Thin Blue Line Act and the Probation Officer Protection Act are minimal more than political acting — acting that we would ill be able to manage the cost of as we manufacture more secure and more joined groups.

CHAPTER FOUR

Women in Law Enforcement

Gender inequality is still a defining aspect of law enforcement, even in today's world of slowly increasing employment fairness. Women comprise only a small percentage of the local law enforcement in agencies across the nation. Though their presence in the police force dates back to the beginning of the 20th century, it's only been noticeable in the past 40 years. In the 1970s, women accounted for roughly 2 percent of sworn officers, with most of the women holding clerical positions. Yet, despite progressive legislation aimed at procuring gender equality in the United States, women today make up only 13 percent of the force, most significantly in larger departments. Women in law enforcement are often inexplicitly resented by their male counterparts and many face harassment.

Additionally, many women encounter a 'brass' ceiling and are unable to rise to supervisory positions despite their qualifications. Many women do not even try to reach these positions because of fear of oppression from male coworkers. Few women receive the guidance necessary to overcome this obstacle; however, the National Association of Women Law Enforcement Executives (NAWLEE) has been working hard since 1995 to mentor women in executive positions and help guide new female officers to grasp the opportunity to achieve these leadership roles. Their president, Commander Kristen Ziman of the Aurora (Illinois) Police Department who has endured the hard process of becoming an executive, shared her experience as a woman in law enforcement and her recommendations to others starting this difficult journey.

When Commander Ziman became a police cadet in 1991, women in the Aurora Police Department had not advanced beyond the rank of patrol officer. While the inequality did not figure into her decision, she also did not aspire to obtain a leadership position. She was conscious of the minority situation, and was the only woman of six officers to enter the department in 1994. While at the police academy, she felt that she and the other women in her position often "needed to prove [them]selves." Whereas their male counterparts were easily accepted, the women were automatically considered inferior and only seemed to be able to change this perception by showing the men otherwise. The women in the academy were watched more closely and felt they were expected to do something incorrectly. Yet, in her experience, the moment that competency was proven, much of the inequality faded away. But some still remained. After three successful months of training, the head of the academy met with Commander Ziman and her Field Training Officer. The FTO was asked if Ziman had ever been in a fight. Ziman had not, but her FTO said that she did not need to prove herself that way because of her ability to talk through a potentially dangerous situation. Ziman was later informed by her FTO that such a question was never asked of the male cadets. Ziman was very fortunate in that there weren't many similar incidents during the course of her career. She simply tried to do her job and do it well, and as a result, her competency was not questioned. Ziman was the first female lieutenant, and later commander, in Aurora city history. According to her, at this level, gender is rarely an issue. Rather, every leader is being watched by both the officers and the general public.

During her years spent rising through the ranks and since attaining her current role, Ziman has helped to promote gender equality. She has done her best to mentor fellow female police officers and, with the help of NAWLEE, has successfully aided women who were motivated to reach the executive level of law enforcement. Though she acknowledges that each gender tends to have special skill sets, the best person for any job should have that job. One skill set women often have is that they are more able to communicate with fellow citizens. Ziman believes that "women really have the gift of influence" and recalled that she had "to talk [her] way out of things" when violence could have ensued. However, Ziman also knows many men who are very good at communicating.

As the president of a mentoring organization, Ziman is tasked with guiding fellow women in law enforcement. In discussing herself and fellow women around her, Ziman expressed fear that "we hold ourselves back." If women do not have the dedication to climb the ranks of law enforcement, they will rarely succeed at making the climb. Women need to "forge [their] own path, [for they] truly are responsible for [their] own career." Yet Ziman understands one of the main reasons why so few women have the necessary aspirations: The hard work hours required of a law enforcement executive do not mix well with family obligations. Ziman often suggests that women find a supportive partner who will help them reach their dreams by easing the strain of the many hard work hours. Although she understands many women's dilemma, she does believe that more women are necessary for a police force to function properly. The police's first priority is to "emulate the community we serve." Thus far, the small percentage of women on the force impedes this from happening.

The discrimination women in law enforcement face today may not be as extreme as it was, but it is still a problem. "Some of it is self-imposed, presently," but improvement is still possible. Ziman recalled that her first FTO was a woman. Without describing the unpleasant events the FTO had experienced in previous years, Ziman noted that it was "unmentionable, the things that happened to her." Also, the men "didn't want her to be there" and would exclude her from office activities. Accordingly, the FTO had developed a strong feeling of resentment toward her profession.

Despite these common past occurrences, Ziman claimed that women today, just like men, are responsible for their own careers. They need to be assertive and listen to the voice inside of them urging them to strive for success. Ziman waited, like many women do, to rise in the ranks. She was told to take the sergeant's test rather than seeking out the opportunity. And many women unfortunately fear being ridiculed by male coworkers if they attempt to reach the executive level.

Since its creation in 1995, NAWLEE has quickly grown into a national organization, guiding and helping women in law enforcement around the country. Its staff, headed by Commander Ziman, is composed of fellow law enforcement executives working to address gender discrimination and end the inequality that pervades the profession.

Advantages of Women in Law Enforcement

It is challenging! When you go to work, you never know what you will be doing that day. It could be taking reports of crimes, counseling a runaway girl, arresting a wanted person, helping an elderly or lost person, or any one of a thousand other things. There is certainly no routine in this job.

It is rewarding! If you like to help people, this could be the job for you. Every day, you are called to assist people in a time of crisis. They turn to you for the help and advice they need. You can make a tremendous impact on their lives. You can help a young child avoid becoming a victim, or an offender. You can help people make their neighborhood a safer place. Every day, you will go home knowing that you have made a difference in someone's life.

Policing today has professional standards and high expectations of those who enter. The police are often the first, and sometimes the only, contact many citizens will have with a government representative. Police actions can influence attitudes about the entire government system.

The Colorado Springs Police Department prides itself on the level of professionalism to which all officers are held. Recruiting women is an integral part of building a police department that is representative of the community it serves.

Today's policing environment is more receptive than ever before to the unique skills that women bring to policing. Yet, there are still myths about women in law enforcement.

Myth: Police applicants need to already know a lot about self-defense, laws and using firearms.

Fact: Many police applicants have no background in any of those things – many have never fired a gun, studied criminal law or done any kind of martial arts. CSPD pays police recruits while they attend about 24 - 26 weeks of training. The training will teach new police officers all of the basic skills needed to be a police officer, such as:

- Constitutional, state and traffic laws
- Defensive tactics and physical training
- Firearms training and defensive driving
- Investigative procedures and report writing
- CSPD policies and procedures
- New technologies

After completing the academy, new officers ride with a Police Training Officer for 15 weeks to begin applying new skills to real-world situations.

Myth: Women aren't thick skinned enough to be good police officers.

Fact: Police Officers are exposed to undesirable and sometimes traumatic incidents. Compassion and empathy during those times serves the community well. Many of the interpersonal skills women traditionally possess are invaluable to effective policing.

Myth: Police work requires people who are physically imposing.

Fact: Police work is not all about size and muscles. You do have to pass a job-related physical ability test, but good general physical conditioning is more important than size or strength.

Myth: It is very difficult to be a mother and a police officer while working varying shifts.

Fact: Shift selection occurs annually. Many CSPD women are working mothers. Some are single mothers.

Myth: Being a female police officer is very different from being a male officer.

Fact: Badges come in gold or silver, not pink or blue. Policing is a challenging and rewarding profession limited only by the abilities of the individual officer. There are thousands of successful women in policing today. As more women have entered the profession, there is greater acceptance among their peers and the public.

Myth: Female police Officers encounter relationship problems with loved ones who cannot accept their chosen profession

Fact: When someone enters a profession that could involve danger, there is some apprehension by those who care about that person. CSPD offers ride-along programs and family education programs that help alleviate the fears of family members by allowing them to see first-hand the amount of backup and support officers receive from peers.

Women in Law Enforcement: Two steps forward, three steps back

In 1845, the first women to be hired by the New York City Police Department were called "matrons." In 1985, Penny Harrington of the Portland Oregon Police Department became the first female Chief of Police, Today, once the last bastion of male domination in the workplace, police organizational attitudes are finally beginning to change. And yet serious problems still remain.

In 2004, women accounted for only 12.7 percent of all sworn law enforcement positions in large agencies and the numbers are declining. The percentage of sworn female officers in smaller agencies is even lower (most agencies in the U.S. have fewer than ten sworn officers.) in spite of women comprising at 46.5 percent of the entire labor force.

There are many possible reasons for the decline in the number of women pursuing careers in law enforcement. Although research shows that women can be just as effective as men, uneven hiring practices, selection processes and recruitment policies keep the number of women artificially low. Often women are screened out of the selection process early on, as a result of certain entry level tests that favor upper body strength or previous life experience, such as military service.

Most women never even consider a career in law enforcement to begin with, due to their misunderstanding of the nature of the job, and the aggressive and authoritarian images portrayed in the media. Once hired, however, women still face discrimination, sexual harassment, or even peer intimidation, and they often lack the necessary role models or mentors to help them move up the ranks. Many never even take promotional exams, giving first priority to family or personal relationships.

All of this thwarts any efforts to recruit and retain more women, and is, in part, why numbers remain stagnant or continue to decline. And yet, recent changes in policing philosophy, emphasizing problem solving and community over intervention, have brought to light glaring inefficiencies and injustices. Widespread excessive force and corruption scandals, overwhelmingly attributed to male officers, are costing cities millions of dollars a year in lawsuit payouts.

Because female officers utilize a different policing style and rely less on physical force and more on communications skills, potentially violent confrontations and are less likely to occur, or escalate into excessive force situations. Thus citizen complaints, or civil liabilities, are substantially less likely to occur. The implications of not having a representative number of female officers is clear.

The under-representation of women at all levels in the modern police agency negatively impacts the culture and operational efficiency of law enforcement agencies throughout the country. Given the many difficult challenges facing modern agencies, the need to hire more women has never been more urgent.

Tactical Differences Between Male and Female Officers

Some of you may have perused the book Men are from Mars, Women are from Venus, by John Gray or the new book now out Why Men Don't Listen and Women Can't Read Maps, by Barbara and Allan Pease. Strikingly the Peases ventured to the far corners of the planet for a long time gathering discoveries of new research on the mind, transformative science and social changes to give a scientific clarification of why men and women are how they are. The book says "Men and Women are different. Worse or more terrible - different. Pretty much the main thing they have in like manner is that they have a place with similar animal types." "Men can never discover a couple of socks, however their CDs are in sequential order arrange. Women can simply locate the missing arrangement of auto keys however once in a while the most direct course to their goal." But how does this identify with the strategic differences amongst male and female officers? How would we bring this information and get down to the genuine stuff? From what I have perused, and additionally from a Caliber Press session I went to at the International Association of Women Police Conference in Denver, there have all the earmarks of being significant police-related differences amongst men and women. Also, it is likely to our greatest advantage as police officers to benefit from the differences and utilizes them further bolstering our good fortune. While on the opposite side, if the differences cause challenges, change our technique for preparing to suit the differences. Here are a few cases:

Sheer size: the little size of a lady takes into consideration better utilization of cover and disguise. They are more adaptable and take into consideration more alternatives amid development or cover. Notwithstanding, women have littler hands than men and may experience issues with a similar size gun. Suck it up and get her a littler gun. Try not to set her up for disappointment the moment she hits the line. Give her the gear she needs to carry out the employment and be effective, rather than giving her a gigantic weapon and saying "I disclosed to you she couldn't cut it."

Women have better vision in low light, better fringe vision and better hearing. They can hear a more extensive scope of sound frequencies and tones in the human voice. This is intended to monitor youngsters - you know, the mother thing. Be that as it may, men have favorable position as women tend to see things far away and are less inclined to see things directly before us. Men see what's directly before them. This is a strategic misstep that ought to be overwhelmed with some sex specific preparing.

Women are better at multitasking; in any case, we need to look out that we don't do three things with average ability as opposed to one thing admirably. Everything in policing must be done to the most noteworthy quality, regardless of whether it is report composing, talking or exploring.

Men have a greater mind. Apologies, women - it's valid. However, women have more nerve cells interfacing the privilege and left cerebrum, which enables us the capacity to backpedal and forward and exchange information from the inventive side to the computational side of our brains, coordinating up our verbal agree with our visual, imaginative side a ton quicker. The reasoning to-the-saying happens speedier. The Caliber Press session depicted it as the women having a "superhighway" between the two sides of the cerebrum, and the men having an "earth street"- - their words, not mine, don't shoot the envoy. This takes into account speedier translation and verbalization of what we see and is a decent quality to have as an officer.

Women can store in their brains a wide range of irregular data. Do you ever recall your wife recollecting - and reminding you- - of everything about each and every battle you've ever had, and what truly matter to it? Yes, we focus on detail. This makes us possibly great examiners and great at taking a gander at an assortment of parts of a wrongdoing, and recollecting that them.

Women are less simple to outrage. The more distressing a circumstance gets, the more quiet we get. Outrage will probably go to a male officer than a female officer (recall, this is summing up from an organic point of view - I've seen heaps of women go on turn cycle and huge amounts of men bear on as though nothing happened). In any case, women have a tendency to falter, as opposed to act with animosity. Female officers should be prepared to overcome that. It is critical in strategic circumstances. It could involve life or death.

There are numerous strategic differences amongst men and women in policing. I've quite recently addressed a couple. Obviously, every individual is different, and these are recently summed up talks. Nonetheless, if you perceive some of these issues in the men or women you are preparing, it would be to your greatest advantage to benefit from their qualities and give preparing to address the shortcomings. Keep in mind, it is imperative to give preparing to fit the individual, instead of treat all officers the same. There might be preparing required for littler officers, be them male or female, because of sheer size. There could be different preparing required for inactive officers instead of your more forceful officers. The business world has identified specific preparing to address the issues of their staff with a specific end goal to make them as effective as could be allowed. They need to- - their benefits rely upon it. All in all, why doesn't policing? It should- - now and then lives rely upon it. One day, that life might be yours. Consider it.

The Benefits of a Career in Law Enforcement

Most attractive careers share some common characteristics including good benefits, promotion opportunity, and salary increases. However, law enforcement offers a few benefits and advantages not readily found in other career paths.

Diversity of Job Options

Law enforcement offers candidates a diverse selection of jobs and career options to choose from. Whether you want to work at the federal, state or local level you'll find a plethora of career options available to pursue. At the local level career options include municipal, corrections officer, private security guard, police officer, investigative officer, court clerk, criminologist, paralegal, and lawyer or even judge. At the state level career options include such jobs as patrol officer, state trooper, state highway patrol, investigative officer, lawyer, judge, and bailiff. At the federal level there are either investigative or uniformed career options to choose from. Investigative-type jobs include positions with the Drug Enforcement Agency (DEA) or the Bureau of Alcohol, Tobacco, Firearms and Explosives (ATF). Uniformed jobs include positions with the Secret Service or Federal Bureau of Investigation (FBI), and other federal law enforcement agencies.

Job Security

Although unfortunate, domestic and international crime is on the rise and security is a major concern for our nation--as well as other nations. Increase in crime, combined with an ever growing population, creates a never ending demand for qualified law enforcement professionals. According to a report released by the U.S. Department of Labor, Bureau of Labor Statistics the demand for qualified law enforcement professionals is expected to continue at a rate higher than that for most other occupations through the year 2018.

Attractive Benefits

In addition to job security, most law enforcement professionals are provided generous pension plans and attractive retirement packages. This is especially true for law enforcement officer working at the federal level. Federal law enforcement officers generally receive annual salary increases and most federal employees receive special salary rates to compensate them for expected overtime and relocation.

Law enforcement availability pay (LEAP), equal to 25 percent of the employee's base salary grade, is provided to federal employees (most frequently federal officers) who are expected to work extended overtime. State and local law enforcement employees are also paid overtime time pay--typically, on a per hour basis.

Many law enforcement officers and employees are also provide special allowance to compensate them for work related traveling, lodging and living expenses.

Many police officer can retire at half-pay (half their base salary) after only 20 years of service and many federal officers and employees can retire at full retirement pay after 20 years in the service. The enables most law enforcement professionals the ability to pursue another exciting career after only 20 years of service if they desire.

Law enforcement and criminal justice careers are in our opinion offer some of the most attractive and rewarding benefits of any career fields. But even if the benefits mentioned above were non-existent a career in law enforcement or criminal justice will still provide you with one of the most exciting and rewarding career experiences available. Professionals who pursue a career in law enforcement and criminal justice do so because they want to, not because they have to.

CHAPTER FIVE

AFRICAN AMERICAN IN LAW ENFORCEMENT

In the mid-1950s, Clarence White was a new kid on the block policeman with the Indianapolis Police Department, and being African-American, there were rules he expected to take after. He says the division had a man of honor's understanding where black cops could not capture white individuals.

White is the patriarch of three eras of African-American police officers in the Indianapolis Police Department. It was a vocation he at first did not need.

"I was kind of constrained into this," says White. "I attempted to join the fire office three times, turned down three times since they said I didn't finish the test."

White credits his tenacious uncle, who was at that point on the police compel, for motivating him to take the police exam. White said it was an indistinguishable inquiries from the fire division test. He go with a 99 percent.

Amid that time, White was just permitted to ride in two police autos — Car 27 and Car 29. Those numbers let general society know African-American police officers were inside.

The Indianapolis office had African-American police officers going back to the 1890s, yet White, now 90, was a piece of the original of African-Americans to make rank. He climbed to commander before resigning in 1974.

In spite of his part in integrating the office, he bent over backward to shield his children from emulating his example. In the mornings, he says he would toss on a jacket to shield his children from seeing his police uniform.

Be that as it may, when his most seasoned child, Clarence White Jr., now 66, joined the compel in 1975, his dad hushed up about his reservations.

White Jr. said he began his profession on the constraint amid the finish of the nonconformist transformation, when police officers were not very much loved. Popular conclusion deteriorated when the division ended up plainly entangled in national embarrassments including inordinate utilization of constraint and the shootings of unarmed black men.

Today, White Jr., thinks police shootings of unarmed black individuals proceeds, to a limited extent, due to bigotry in the office.

"I've been included in a circumstance where a white officer ... I felt his enormous issue in working in the community was his aversion of black individuals. It exists. It will dependably exist and is something that we need to persistently progress in the direction of improving," he says.

His nephew Rodney White, 41, likewise says it will take some work, however, these issues can be settled.

Rodney is as yet dynamic in the Indianapolis Police Department. Growing up, he was encompassed by police officers, including his mom and dad.

With regards to managing police shootings of unarmed black individuals. He said it will require all the more preparation and an emphasis on enrolling more officers from the community.

"If you don't experience childhood in a specific area, and you're not used to managing the African-American culture and a portion of the characteristics and the way that we talk and the way that we convey ourselves ... You need to really associate with it to truly sort of comprehend," Rodney says.

In spite of endeavors by police offices across the country to utilize more non-white individuals into the drive, African-Americans still hold a more horrible perspective of police than their white partners, as indicated by Pew Research.

Clarence White Sr., says this perspective is an issue African-American officers still need to explore while they're in the field.

"Black men and women on the road — when they go up against a white officer, it's with the feeling that what they say or how they say it, will imprison. What's more, the black officers, a similar thing happens," he says. "We put on a uniform, and the black community says you speak to the white foundation. So we have an issue attempting to prevail upon them."

Be that as it may, White Sr. has an approach he utilized before he resigned.

"When I moved toward a white culprit or a black culprit, I whispered to him what I would do," says White. Sr. "I didn't constrain anyone — punch him, anything."

He says it's the means by which he would have jumped at the chance to be dealt with.

African American Police Officers were selected to Police Departments in the late 1860's:

1867: Selma, Alabama

1868: Jackson, Florida

1870: Houston and Galveston, Texas

1870: New Orleans, Louisiana had 177 African American Officers and three of five Police Board individuals were African American.

April 12, 1870: Officer William Johnson of Jacksonville, Florida turns into the primary perceived African American police officer murdered in the line of obligation.

1875: Bass Reeves was selected as the principal African American Deputy U.S. Marshal

1916: Georgia Ann Robinson turned into the principal African American lady police officer. She served in the Los Angeles Police Department.

1928: Dr. Louis Tompkins Wright is the main know African American Police Surgeon. He later progressed toward becoming President of the NAACP Board of Directors

1941: William B. Lindsay turned into the main known African American State Trooper, contracted by the Illinois State Police.

1966: Sheriff Lucius Amerson was one for the main chose African American Sheriffs. He filled in as Sheriff of Macon County, Alabama.

1972: National Black Police Association was sanctioned

1976: National Organization of Black Law Enforcement Executive (NOBLE) was established.

1988: Willie L. Williams ends up plainly one of the primary African American Police Commissioners. He served in Philadelphia and in this way turned into the principal African American Police Commissioner of Los Angeles Police Department in 1992.

History of Mistrust

African Americans are less trusting of law enforcement in Los Angeles County, poll finds

Despite two decades of efforts to improve relations, Los Angeles County law enforcement is still struggling to build trust among African American residents, according to a new poll.

Leaders at the Los Angeles Police Department and other agencies have diversified their ranks, changed tactics and launched community programs in hopes of shedding a longstanding image among some black residents that authorities treat them unfairly – efforts that have drawn praise from others.

But the new survey, published Tuesday by the Center for the Study of Los Angeles at Loyola Marymount University, revealed mixed reviews of law enforcement in Los Angeles County, with the greatest skepticism coming from African Americans.

About half of the 2,425 L.A. County residents polled rated the quality of their police services, along with the conduct and professionalism of officers, as “good,” according to the survey’s results.

But when African Americans were asked to rate police, the percentages dropped. About a quarter of African Americans polled considered the conduct and professionalism of officers "good." About a third — 31.5% — described officers' behavior as "poor." The rest said it was "fair."

When asked how confident they were that police in their communities treated all races equally, just over 42% of the black residents surveyed said they were "not confident," compared with 30% of Latinos polled, 25% of whites and nearly 20% of Asian Americans.

Regardless of what the call for service is, we are there to be the protectors, the guardians of the community," Rivero said. "We need to leave that contact where the person who calls us feels that we were there to help them. Every single day, that has to occur.

Ernest Spradley, who is African-American, says he chuckled when the south suburban white cop who pulled him over told him he was going 95 mph down a main drag.

Many black officers say they very much understand the conditions that brought young people to the streets to protest harsh treatment by officers, white and black. But they bristle at attacks on police at a time when violent crime in Chicago is a national topic.

"There are good and bad in every profession, any profession, and I don't deny we have bad cops," said a black veteran patrol officer assigned to the majority black Wentworth police District on the South Side, who asked not to be identified. "But what offends me the most is the protests like they're doing now. A possibly bad shooting happens somewhere else in the country — where is your protest over the 4-year-old who was just shot?"

Police work, racial solidarity

The handful of black officers reached by the Tribune say angry exchanges with loved ones and strangers regarding their police work are rare, though they can occur, especially after high-profile brutality cases in the news.

Fletcher can still recall the heated exchange with a close friend involving the death of LaTanya Haggerty, an unarmed African-American woman who was shot and killed in summer 1999 by a Chicago police officer who mistook her cellphone for a weapon.

One of my non-police friends," Fletcher began, "he's like, 'Man how can you stand up behind that? Because they just killed that girl and she just had a cellphone. That could have been you or me, your sister, your little cousin.

The public doesn't look at the other end. What if it wasn't a cellphone?" he said. "What if it was a gun? And police officers have to make that split (second) decision, because you say I can wait to see if it's a cellphone and be killed. The average officer isn't willing to take that chance with their life.

Black cops know how volatile things can be at a crime scene. But while they may face the same dangers as white officers, some black residents — be they witnesses, victims or even the accused — may open up more freely to a black officer than their white counterparts, some black cops have observed.

Sometimes the victim may look to a familiar face and hear a little bit more clearer from a familiar face," said Spradley, who grew up in the Grand Crossing neighborhood and graduated from Morehouse College. "They're more apt to hear what the familiar face is saying when the other (white) officer may have told them pretty much the same thing.

Black officers interviewed by the Tribune say they're as concerned as anyone about the abuse and callousness some of their white counterparts have toward African-Americans. They've faced it. Their family, friends and neighbors have complained about it.

But the officers say they don't have the political muscle to make changes. And they're preoccupied with a skyrocketing shooting and homicide rate.

Police shooting deaths of African-Americans locally and nationally are further putting black officers on defense forced to answer for the actions of fellow law enforcement officers.

Officers say they feel blindsided with the release of every new viral video showing an attack on a black civilian.

The negative is often every day because there's something new popping up every day in the news," said the Wentworth District officer who asked not to be identified.

Getting past echoes of Jim Crow laws

Fletcher is among those officers who has deep concerns about policing in minority communities, while he also questions the media's treatment of the problem and the community's response.

"If you just looked at the media, you would think that the biggest issue for black folks is police brutality. But if you took a bloody weekend, all you've got to do is look at the number of people shot by police and the number of black people shot by black folks, and the (police) number pales in comparison."

Fletcher was one of a number of officers bothered by police actions seen in videos of the arrest of Chicago-area native Sandra Bland, who died in a Texas jail last year, as well as the 16-shot death of Laquan McDonald in Chicago.

Starting out as a Chicago cop at 22 in the late 1980s, Fletcher said he's seen the good, bad and ugly of police work and has always been troubled by some white colleagues who lacked empathy for the black residents they serve.

"There are a lot of white officers who really didn't see that (McDonald's death) was overkill," Fletcher said. "I wouldn't say that all of the white officers, or even the average one, has no empathy. But I would say a lot of them don't have any empathy and at times they don't even understand that they don't. But in the things that they say, you see it."

Some older black officers say a lack of understanding and some heavy-handed, old school policing tactics decried by activists and black cops alike have historic roots in Jim Crow segregation and persist to this day in some communities.

"It was a way you were raised and brought up. The officers that came in our community who were not black wanted you to fear them," said Greg Baker, a regional vice president of the National Organization for Black Law Enforcement Executives, who is also the police chief in South Holland. "It was like, if you were afraid of us, we can keep you in line. You would do whatever we tell you or not, whether it was for your benefit or not."

Police work is more than policing

Some retired cops are hoping these most recent police incidents will shine a light on the need to hire more black officers in the city. Only about 23 percent of officers in Chicago are African-American, compared with the city's black population of 32 percent.

Patricia Hill, former head of the African American Police League, says the city desperately needs black officers who embrace their heritage and are devoted to providing service to communities in need.

You need police officers who can change hats," she said, adding that in black communities, cops sometimes "have to become the social worker, the teacher. ... It's not just about kicking a-- and taking names. It's a service, you're a public service employee. And in the black community, 90 percent of your calls are service calls.

People are not getting along. And you have to be able to negotiate that. Many of the white officers in the black community don't see black people as needing service. They need to be policed: 'Y'all don't know how to act, you need to be put in order, talked down to, civilized' and all that. That's why you have this adversarial relationship. We need more officers that give service. When you call the police, you want help and that's what we need.

Spradley says that long-ago traffic stop that ended with an official warning from the suburban cop is a reminder how police must work harder to maintain a respectful relationship with the people they serve.

He says he tries to hold on to the memory of what it was like to be robbed multiple times as a teen while traveling from his South Side home to Providence St. Mel Catholic High School on the West Side.

I want to be the police officer that responds when my coat gets snatched off my back, or somebody's chasing me down a street to get my gym shoes off my feet. I wanted to be that police officer that gave the service that I would want to have if I was the victim — and I had been the victim.

CHAPTER SIX

LBGT IN LAW ENFORCEMENT

The involvement of LGBTQ officers in law enforcement has a background marked by contention. As circumstances are different, police powers have adjusted by including LGBTQ divisions, officers and boards inside their positions to represent enactment built up by governments to secure people who beforehand had practically no voice when it came to laws affecting their own groups.

Diversity and consideration in policing

Diversity in benefit and the disposal of separation over the planet is driven by numerous people, staff, affiliations and others inside the worldwide police community.

In any case, numerous LGBTQ people still face significant segregation in the police constrain. In a 2013 investigation of British strengths, Jones and Williams found that just about 20% of sexual minority officers said they encountered segregation. In the meantime, just 25% of those people announced the episode to a prevalent, 5% of those people revealed the occurrence to an administrator.

Lesbian, Gay, Bisexual and Transgender (LGBT) individuals in law enforcement confront unavoidable segregation. The new report refreshes a 2009 give an account of segregation in broad daylight business, which found that more than 40 percent of the revealed instances of separation happened against law enforcement and remedies office faculty. This refreshed report audits confirmation of victimization 95 law enforcement and adjustments representatives since 2000.

Key discoveries include:

- The segregation experienced frequently went past terminating or downgrade and included serious verbal badgering and lewd behavior, including a demise danger, prejudicial slurs, foul presentation and improper touching.

- Many of the reports uncovered physical provocation or brutality towards the officers. These included reports of being hammered into a solid divider, assaulted with a seat, and rehashed reports of officers being declined go down, putting their own wellbeing in risk.

- Over 66% of LGBT law enforcement officers in a recent report revealed hearing homophobic remarks at work and over half detailed being dealt with like a pariah by their partners.

- A current overview of 60 individuals from TCOPS, an association for transgender law enforcement officers, found that more than 90% announced negative encounters with their specializations.

- Surveys on non-LGBT officers additionally record high rates of unfair states of mind. For instance, a recent report found that of overviewed police boss in Texas more than one of every four "demonstrated that they would experience issues working with a gay man," and roughly half would experience issues working with a lesbian officer.

There are exactly 9.5 million LGBT individuals in the United States, where homosexuality laws existed in each state until 1961.

It wasn't until 2003 that the U.S. Preeminent Court pronounced those laws to be unlawful.

There still isn't a government arrangement that completely bans separation in view of genuine or saw sexual introduction and sex personality, as indicated by the report.

Law enforcement in the United States has a background marked by abusing the LGBT community and separation and provocation keep on being inescapable, the report said.

Study information, and also singular declarations and accounts, examined in the UCLA overview showed how segregation and mishandle by police officers prompted a debilitating trust in law enforcement inside the LGBT community and brought about less wrongdoings being accounted for to the experts.

A current report referred to in the report found that 40 percent of gay and indiscriminate male survivors of aggressive behavior at home trusted the police would be unhelpful or extremely unhelpful. Fifty-nine percent thought police would be more useful to a hetero lady in a similar circumstance.

Another illustration referred to in the UCLA overview is that of a transgender lady in Boston who settled a case with the nearby police office in 2013 after she was captured supposedly to use the women's restroom at a destitute safe house.

She additionally claimed that, after officers took her to the police station, they constrained her to evacuate her shirt and bra and bounce all over while they criticized her.

An exceptional team on policing, set up by President Barack Obama after late real conflicts amongst police and nearby groups in Missouri and New York, discharged proposals went for shutting rifts amongst police and the communities they serve.

"Many police powers have actualized their own inner non-separation arrangements and trainings and strategies on communications with transgender individuals to avoid badgering," Amira Hasenbush, co-creator of the report, told the Thomson Reuters Foundation in an email.

"These are positively ventures the correct way, yet the still elevated amounts of announced separation and badgering demonstrate that there is still much work to be done here."

Racist Police Brutality Is an LGBT Issue

The most recent weeks have been inundated with slugs, blood, and tears in America. From the killing of 49 for the most part LGBT Latinos/as at the Pulse dance club in Orlando, to the butcher of evidently honest youthful Black men on account of police, to the death of five police officers by a disturbed expert marksman at a generally serene challenge in Dallas — the most recent month has abandoned us all things considered in stun, in misery, and longing to comprehend it all.

There are some consistent ideas that line together the majority of the current upsetting occasions into profitable lessons that, if paid attention to, will clear our way ahead.

We require a great deal more sensible direction of firearm ownership and utilize, including the arrival of the attack weapons boycott. We require clearer and more sensible norms for the use of deadly drive by police — benchmarks that allow the utilization of lethal constraint just when totally important to secure the life of the officer or others adjacent. We require all the more innovatively propelled police apparatuses that cripple yet don't demolish. Also, we require steady and enforceable across the nation preparing for police serving communities of color.

Our diversity as a country is our greatest quality, additionally now and again our greatest test. We should learn, as Americans, to comprehend and value each other better. To connect our differences with what we share. To kill detest with expectation and sympathy. Furthermore, most particularly, to perceive that now and again we see difference and separation where, in all actuality, there just is solidarity and shared involvement.

Solidarity

In the wake of the suspicious and disturbing police killings of Alton Sterling and Philando Castile, Chad Griffin, the leader of the Human Rights Campaign, tweeted: "Similarly as NAACP stood w/us after Orlando, we stand w/them in requesting responsibility for the homicides of Alton Sterling and Philando Castile."

This was a solid proclamation of solidarity with the NAACP originating from the pioneer of the most unmistakable association in the country advancing equity for lesbian, gay, indiscriminate, and transgender individuals. It was a particularly welcome articulation of partnership in light of the American LGBT rights development's long-term battle to perceive and grasp the racial, ethnic, and different types of diversity that helped fuel it since its origin.

As commendable as it might have been, Mr. Griffin's message still imparted a separation — a detachment — that does not truly exist between African Americans and LGBT Americans. We are remaining with them "similarly as" they remained with us? They are Black. We are... what? Not Black? Huh?

Obviously, actually, there is no such detachment. There are incalculable Black individuals, including savage straight partners, in the LGBT development, and there are numerous LGBT individuals in the racial equity development — including in charge of Black Lives Matter and related activities. LGBT African Americans flourish. The LGBT community mirrors the rainbow. The rainbow signal, actually, is a fitting image of our diverse development.

Maybe perceiving the obviously unintentional "Black v. LGBT" removing in his prior tweet, Mr. Griffin later tweeted, impeccably: "The LGBTQ community is as various as the texture of our country. Furthermore, viciousness went for any of us is brutality pointed whatsoever of us." Yes.

"Not Isolated Incidents"

The cell phone recordings catching a report of the last snapshots of the lives of Alton Sterling and Philando Castile have created across the country shock. The recordings themselves, and in addition the records of witnesses, emphatically propose that the police killings of the two men were unjustified. Examinations are in progress and general society anticipates the full subtle elements of the two killings, however from the plenteous confirmation now on general visibility it creates the impression that neither one of the mans represented a danger to the lives of the individual police officers, neither one of the mans displayed a weapon, and neither one of the mans demand to kick the bucket. More terrible yet, as President Obama himself perceived on July seventh, "these deadly shootings are not disconnected occurrences" but rather "symptomatic of the more extensive difficulties inside our criminal equity framework, the racial differences that show up over the framework a seemingly endless amount of time, and the subsequent absence of assume that exists between law enforcement and an excessive number of the communities they serve."

The measurements are calming. A 2015 Guardian examine found that the "rate of police-included deaths" for youthful African-American guys "was five times higher than for white men of a similar age." a similar report noticed that roughly a fourth of the Black individuals killed by police were not equipped (rather than just 17 percent of whites). Also, these are quite recently the extraordinary cases. Toward the end of last year, the University of Chicago's Center for the Study of Race, Politics, and Culture discharged an investigation recording that well finished portion of African-American youngsters revealed being the objective of police badgering or mishandle or knowing somebody who had been the casualty of such bigot policing.

The proof is unquestionable that the connection between the American law enforcement community and African Americans is on a very basic level more beset, and of a completely different nature than the connections amongst police and alternate groups they serve. While numerous Americans see police as wellsprings of well-being, security, and solace, numerous African Americans see police as speaking to accurately the inverse. Unfortunately, as appeared by the plenty of proof over such a large number of years, the doubt is not without premise.

Another Symptom of the Same Malaise

African Americans have borne the greater part of the brunt of police mercilessness. However, injurious policing is not outsider to the LGBT community for the most part. LGBT Americans of all races have for some time been hassled and brutalized by narrow-minded police. It was police assaults like those at L.A's. Cooper's Donuts in 1959 and the Stonewall Inn in 1969, actually that quickened the development for LGBT rights. When it was illegal to serve mixed beverages to gay individuals, and for gay individuals to move —

don't bother engage in sexual relations — with each other, gay social foundations the nation over were simple and incessant focuses for police badgering. Not unintentionally, these reactant occasions in the LGBT development happened amidst also powerful occasions in the African-American social liberties development.

Under the watchful eye of the Supreme Court, discredited homosexuality laws as illegal in its 2003 Lawrence v. Texas choice, states could criminalize gay sex and, as a result, gay personality. Many did, prompting the absolute abuse of LGBT Americans by police as a "criminal" component, even in those purviews without an enforceable homosexuality law on the books.

Police provocation and mishandle of LGBT individuals, however, particularly Black and Latino/ LGBTs, perseveres as a common issue. In a March 2015 report, UCLA's Williams Institute reasoned that "[d]iscrimination and badgering by law enforcement in view of sexual introduction and sex character is a progressing and unavoidable issue in LGBT people group" and that "such provocation and segregation is most noteworthy for LGBT minorities, transgender people and youth."

Indeed, even after Lawrence struck them down as completely illegal, the proceeding with nearness of homosexuality laws in many state criminal codes has energized homophobic and transphobic police officers to pester and manhandle LGBT individuals the country over today — going so far as capturing and subjecting gay and transgender individuals to costly, debasing, and trivial lawful procedures.

As Joey L. Investor, Andrea J. Ritchie and Kay Whitlock report in their book, Queer (In)Justice: The Criminalization of LGBT People in the United States (Beacon Press, 2012), LGBT Americans have been the casualties of harsh policing in numerous aspects of our lives. From "scurrilous lead" captures following police entanglements, to the provocation of sex non-conforming LGB or transgender individuals for utilizing the "erroneous" restroom or wearing "sexual orientation unseemly" garments. From injurious policing of transgender women for "strolling while trans," to the assault of LGBT sex specialists by police officers themselves, and, at last, to the murdering of trans individuals on account of police - even, on account of a handicapped transgender man, as of late as February 2016.

"Poise and Respect" for All

In this way, we are reminded that bigot police fierceness without a doubt is LGBT development issue, both on the grounds that numerous individuals from our community are Black and dark colored and in light of the fact that the LGBT community all in all, as well, knows the injury of oppressive policing. In an Op-Ed a year ago entitled "It's Time though LGBT People Could not care less

About Police Brutality," Black LGBT lobbyist Samantha Master expressed: "The quest for equity is not finished until the point that each person — paying little heed to their identity — is treated with nobility and regard." She's privilege. In a different piece, Esperanza Garcia and Ty Brooks kept in touch with: "It's the ideal opportunity for every one of us to respect the LGBT community's own rich inheritance of challenge and resistance against police fierceness." I concur.

The youthful Black men who have kicked the bucket on account of police most as of late show up not to have been individuals from the LGBT community. However, their deaths hit home to a significant number of us who likewise have been the objectives of partial policing. Racist policing debilitates all Americans who have been at the brunt of mercilessness and bias in law enforcement. It is another manifestation of a similar issue — another side effect of a similar discomfort.

Racist police fierceness undermines all Americans, irrespective of race and sexual introduction and sex character, who rely upon a reasonable and impartial police constraint to keep, advance and model peace. It tosses into question the authenticity of our lawful framework. It taints our social compact. It imperils our extremely progress as a people. What's more, we should put an end to it. Together, and now.

Improving the Law Enforcement Response to LGBT-Identified Individuals

Some sobering statistics help to illustrate the importance of these issues and the urgent need for additional work in this arena. This summer, the U.S. Centers for Disease Control and Prevention (CDC) published the first-ever nationwide survey on the health risks faced by lesbian, gay, and bisexual (LGB) youth, which includes important statistics on how this population is disproportionately affected by crime. Of the 1.3 million U.S. high school students who identify as gay, lesbian, or bisexual, the survey found that nearly 18 percent have been forced to have sex, compared to about 5 percent of their heterosexual peers. Bisexual and gay students were also twice as likely to have experienced physical violence, sexual dating violence, and bullying. The CDC report also documented the levels of sexual violence, other than rape, that the following populations have experienced in their lifetimes:

- 1 in 8 lesbian women (13.1%)
- Nearly half of bisexual women (46.1%)
- Nearly half of bisexual men (47.4%)
- 4 in 10 gay men (40.2%)

The statistics for LGBT college students are similarly concerning. In January, the Bureau of Justice Statistics and the Office on Violence Against Women released the Campus Climate Survey Validation Study (CCSVS). Through surveys of 25,000 students across 9 demographically diverse schools, the study confirmed previous statistics about campus sexual assault: that on average, more than 1 in 5 (21%) female students experience sexual assault in college, with a significant number of those assaults occurring in the beginning of the academic year; and that 34 percent of college women reported experiencing sexual assault in their lifetimes. But the CCSVS study also provided new data regarding LGBT students, where the news was even worse:

EXPERIENCED SEXUAL ASSAULT IN COLLEGE:

- 28% of transgender women
- 35% of bisexual women

EXPERIENCED SEXUAL ASSAULT IN LIFETIME:

- 46% of transgender women
- 59% of bisexual women
- 42% of gay men and lesbian women

At the White House and throughout the federal government, we are working to foster a better understanding of what these statistics mean for the LGBT community and translating this knowledge into effective prevention and response strategies. DOJ's Guidance on "Identifying and Preventing Gender Bias in Law Enforcement Response to Sexual Assault and Domestic Violence," described in last week's blog, is one such response. The guidance presents ways for police officers to recognize and address biases, assumptions, and stereotypes about victims. For example, it explains that not all victims of gender-based violence are female, not all perpetrators are male, and, not all intimate partner violence is exclusive to heterosexual relationships. Using the DOJ guidance as a basis for developing trainings, protocols, and improved supervision, can be especially useful to law enforcement when engaging with LGBT survivors, who may not initially feel safe in coming forward to law enforcement with reports about violence in their relationships.

Additionally, the Administration is working with communities across the country to advance recommendations of the President's Task Force on 21st Century Policing that bear on these issues. The Task Force's final report made recommendations on policy and oversight, training and education practices, and other strategies to address implicit bias and improve cultural responsiveness to the LGBT community. These recommendations include the establishment of policies that (1) prohibit profiling and discrimination based on gender, gender identity/expression and sexual orientation, and (2) that incorporate early training for recruits, as well as top-down training for all officers, on cultural diversity that includes specific responsiveness to LGBT and gender non-conforming individuals. (These policies may include many of the principles in the Identifying and Preventing Gender Bias in Law Enforcement Response to Sexual Assault and Domestic Violence Guidance.)

DOJ has also hosted various convenings, such as a Roundtable on Identifying and Preventing Gender-Bias in Law Enforcement

Response to Sexual Assault and Domestic Violence (hosted by the Office on Violence Against Women) and a Forum on Gender, Sexuality, and 21st Century Policing (hosted by the Office of Community Oriented Policing Services (COPS)), that have brought together police executives, subject matter experts, and advocates from across the country to discuss specific strategies, best practices, and policies related to policing and the challenges of gender identity and protecting the rights of women and LGBT people. Also, the White House Task Force to Protect Students from Sexual Assault, co-chaired by the Office of the Vice President and the White House Council on Women and Girls, is working to address the impact of gender violence on all students—including those who identify as LGBT—and to provide schools and law enforcement with practical help to develop effective, compassionate, and respectful approaches to addressing these issues.

Finally, from a data perspective, we need to ensure that we are continuing to capture the full dimensions of law enforcement response to LGBT individuals and any trends over time. In 2012, the Attorney General announced that the FBI would begin employing a revised definition of rape used in the collection of national crime statistics, ensuring that rape will be more accurately reported by state and local communities in the FBI's Uniform Crime Reporting System (UCR). Importantly, the revised UCR definition is more inclusive of sexual assault against men, bisexual, and transgender individuals. The systematic collection of this data over time will guide the development of smart and effective policy responses.

About LGBT Rights

Democratic presidential candidate Hillary Clinton and her running mate, Senator Tim Kaine, have been promoting community policing efforts that encourage police officers to go out into their communities and develop new partnerships. But we must also encourage more community members to reach out to law enforcement. Helping officers truly understand and appreciate the people they serve will help break down barriers and mistrust.

I am a firm believer that most Americans—and most police officers—are good people who want to do the right things to protect our children and communities.But sometimes our biases can blind us. And sometimes law enforcement can stumble in developing and implementing policies because they have not had the opportunity to learn from experts and families in their community. Below the surface, there are still too many fears about race, religion, sexual orientation and gender that can fester and stop real progress toward full equality for every American.

I know firsthand because my fears kept me from supporting my own child, who is transgender. I was forced to explore my deepest fears so I could protect my children. Doing so helped me become a better father, a better man and a better citizen.

Our nation needs to do the same. Children and adults of every race, religion, sexual orientation and gender need to know we are willing and able to face our fears and embrace positive change. The first step requires that every law enforcement officer, politician, community leader and parent dig deep and ask, "What am I afraid of?" Facing these fears can be powerful and life-changing.

Not long ago Brock Caton, the Police Chief at the University of Maine at Farmington, reached out to me and asked if I would be willing to come to his department and conduct LGBTQ training for his officers. Shortly thereafter he asked me if the local town police, county police and county correctional officers could attend. I said, "the more the merrier."

I am not a police officer. I am just a parent who has struggled with raising a child whom many people in our country are not ready to support. My child happens to be transgender. There are other parents who are struggling to keep their children safe because their children are African American or Muslim or just perceived as being different. We all need to reach out to law enforcement agencies and ask for an opportunity to tell our stories, to make it real for the officers in the room, to prepare them for the hard discussions and the easy answers that can come when we break through fears we might not even know we have.

I have had the opportunity to participate in a few Civil Rights Training classes conducted by the Department of Justice, and I recently was a contributing writer for a new set of resources, "Police Perspectives: Building Trust in a Diverse Nation," a three-volume set of training materials on increasing cultural awareness, serving diverse communities and building trust. Working with these people gave me the confidence to agree to take even a bigger step forward into the law enforcement community and bare my soul.

To be successful, I knew I would need help. I invited the Associate Dean of Students from the University of Southern Maine, Sarah Holmes to join me in the training and provide much-needed expertise.

When you arrive and stare into the faces of men and women in uniform, it can be a bit intimidating. I started by showing them images of me running a trapline in Alaska, trout fishing in Wyoming and hunting moose in Maine, all designed to reveal that we have much in common. Then I showed them photos of my identical twin baby boys, quickly showing our family transition as our little boy proved that he was really our beautiful daughter

Nicole. With each slide, I became more emotional. During that transition, my family faced many hardships from bullying, harassment, discrimination and serious enough threats that we had to move and live in hiding. I apologized for my emotional displays, but every person in the room was engaged. I recognized their hearts were as visible as their badges, and they were ready to listen.

At the end, there were many questions, strong handshakes and a few hugs. I felt that every one of us in the room had learned something that was going to help our communities grow. I was very proud of every law enforcement officer in that room, and I was so pleased to have had the opportunity to be asked into their home to open a powerful dialogue for change. I called my wife Kelly on the way home and said we had made some new and powerful friends tonight; our kids have some new allies who have new tools that our communities need to grow.

So often community policing focuses on the police sharing their tools while they reach out attempting to build new relationships. I hope there are other Police Chiefs like Brock Caton who will have the courage to reverse roles and let parents and community experts on race, religion, sexual orientation and gender share their tools in our police departments and jails. We must send the message that everyone is welcome.

CHAPTER SEVEN

RELIGIOUS DEMOGRAPHIC IN LAW ENFORCEMENT

Religion or Divine Command Theory

Religion is often considered the most widely used system to make ethical decisions and to conduct moral reasoning (Pollock, 2007). Throughout the world, people rely on a variety of religions to help them determine the most ethical action to take. While divine command theory is widely used throughout the world, there are differences: the application of the theory may differ from religion to religion, and it may differ within each religion.

One of the basic tenets for divine command theory is to use God as the source for all principles. In this way, to rely upon divine command theory, a person must believe that there is a willful and rational god that has provided the direction toward an ethical outcome. It is from God's commands that actions are determined to be right or wrong and, because of this, divine command theory provides an objective assessment of what is ethical or moral.

However, there is ambiguity in the way in which some scripture is interpreted.

There are four assumptions of divine command theory:

i. There is a god.
ii. God commands and forbids certain acts.
iii. An action is right if God commands it.
iv. People ascertain what God commands or forbids.

Divine command theory also provides an explanation of why ethics and morality are so important. In religions, good acts are rewarded in the afterlife, while bad acts condemn the perpetrator to an everlasting punishment. What essentially makes religion such an incredibly powerful ethical system is that there is the spectre of a potentially eternal punishment in the afterlife (Pollock, 2007). This notion of eventual punishment reinforces in its followers the necessity to make ethical decisions based on the commands of their god.

How can divine command theory assist law enforcement in moral dilemmas?

It is important for law enforcement officers who do not practise religion to be cognizant of the importance of religion with believers. As religions provide the most commonly used ethical systems in the world, law enforcement personnel, regardless of their own beliefs, must be aware that not only will some officers refer to scripture, so too will members of the public. It is at times difficult for non-believing officers to understand the power of religion and the importance of its meaning to believers. Non-believers must be cognizant of situations in which, to them, decisions based on divine command theory may seem odd or unethical, but are ethical to the believer. This does not mean that the law does not apply, but that care must be taken to act with empathy when dealing with these situations.

Generally, for officers who believe in God, a source of comfort may be present when facing death or other traumatic events that non-believers may not experience. Officers dealing with death may find comfort in the belief that those who die may be in a better place, that their soul is eternal, and that death may mean that the soul goes to heaven. Believing that death is not the end, but a new beginning, may help officers who practise religion deal with pain and suffering.

Officers are routinely involved in circumstances in which situations appear to be unfair and where innocent bystanders are victimized with tragic outcomes. Officers who believe in God are also able to look at these situations and find comfort in the belief that God has a plan for everyone, even those who have been unfairly victimized. These officers can draw strength from their belief that the apparently random victimization wasn't so random, and that God was acting in a way that, while hard to explain, is planned for some reason only known to God.

Specifically, divine command theory can offer officers a written or prescribed direction to morality. Officers who are faced with a situation in which their values clash with society may fall back on divine command theory for direction in grey areas. An officer who is surrounded with unethical activity by officers, other criminal justice workers, and people on the street may be able to withstand pressure to join in the immoral practice with the belief that God commands moral behaviour toward everyone and prohibits such things as theft through corruption.

Officers could also use divine command theory to reaffirm in their own minds what is right, even when the Criminal Code or other legislation is unclear on a particular issue. By officers asking themselves what would God command or prohibit, they may be able to make a decision that they can justify.

Finally, officers who believe that God is always good would therefore believe that all of God's commands and prohibitions are good. By interpreting scripture, following the directions of religious authority, or making individual interpretations of God's command and prohibitions, officers are therefore able to do good, understanding that ultimately it is God's commands that they follow, and therefore their actions are good.

Criticisms of Divine Command Theory

While religion may be the most common ethical system employed, it has many issues that can be problematic if used as a moral guideline for law enforcement officers. For law enforcement officers in a pluralistic society, who are entrenched in religious doctrine and make ethical decisions based on that religious doctrine, their ethical decisions will not be acceptable with numerous segments of the society that they are sworn to treat equally. While decisions based on religious doctrine may be satisfactory for a law enforcement officer in his or her personal life, they can create difficulties in the workplace. An example is a law enforcement officer who refuses to enforce a court order to clear a group of Christians protesting abortion. The Christian officer may take offecse to such an order, in spite of the court's ruling and society's general acceptance of abortion.

Specifically, in a criminal justice context, Rawls (2005) viewed religion in public life as something that was out of place and that should, instead, be a private affair. Our religious and personal morals should be put aside when doing the business of the public. It is important, according to Rawls, that workers in government institutions not demonstrate their religious affiliations because we all receive benefits from living in a pluralistic society and that, as a result, we ought to withhold our religious and personal morals to ensure equality.

Other criticisms of divine command theory include:

Religious scriptures are generally ancient and are hard to interpret against the complexities of today's society. As a result, religion as an ethical system does not provide specific ethical guidance to specific ethical dilemmas. Scriptures are ambiguous and are generally broad in nature.

There are many religions in the world, with each possessing different prescriptions for morality. Religions have different gods from one another that are worshipped. Does the god a person chooses make a difference? Can you pray to the "wrong" god, or no god?

Science has no evidence of the existence of God. Without a belief in the existence of God, divine command theory loses its authority among a large portion of the population who base their lives on science and empiricism.

If we do believe in God, "who" determines what the commands are is not absolutely known or agreed upon. Within religious sects, arguments about who interprets commands is commonly a schism that separates factions.

Those who believe in God can interpret the commands in their own way, thereby creating different interpretations to the solutions sought for ethical dilemmas; consequently, there can be confusion about what exactly is God's will.

Contradictions in scripture are confusing. On one side there is mention of the sanctity for life, but there are interpretations that are cited by fundamentalists that provide allowances to cause death to other humans. The most commonly used example of this is in the Quran, in which one passage reads that infidels are to be caught and slayed, but another preaches that Allah loves transgressors. Interestingly, the first verse, it is argued by Muslims, is taken out of context, and refers to Muslims providing self-defence. Interpretations as to what constitutes self-defence further complicates when this verse should be enacted. Should an infidel, in the eyes of a fundamentalist, be slayed for what the fundamentalist deems as an insult, and therefore an attack?

The notion that the might or power of God should be the basis of our ethical decisions indicates that the morality of the decision is based upon the fear of God's might and power. If this is so, then is the decision really an ethical decision, or is it coerced?

Time is upon law enforcement to adapt and accept change

In a gesture to the developing number of South Asian Sikhs in New York City, the Police Department said recently that it would permit officers who have a place with the religion to wear beards and turbans while in uniform — as long as the turbans are blue.

The choice puts the country's biggest police drive among a little gathering of law enforcement agencies like those of Washington, D.C., and Riverside, Calif., and also the United States Army, that enable individuals to have facial hair and wear turbans, regularly as a religious special case. The Royal Canadian Mounted Police has permitted turbans and facial hair since the 1990s and started allowing hijabs this year.

As per the watch guide of the New York Police Department, officers are disallowed from having whiskers and nonuniform hoods, yet exemptions can be made for officers who get a therapeutic or religious settlement to wear facial hair up to one millimeter long, basically stubble.

While the office has turned out to be more assorted, numerous activists say the strategies have harmed the office's objective of being more comprehensive. What's more, the division consented to audit its facial hair rules after a Muslim officer documented a government legal lawsuit in June. That case is pending.

Under the updated arrangement, Commissioner James P. O'Neill said, officers who are conceded a religious settlement from the division's Equal Employment Opportunity Office will be permitted to have whiskers that reach out up to one-half crawl from the face. The officers may likewise wear turbans — with a cap shield it joined to it — set up of the customary police top.

Newcomers of the New York Police Department praised their graduation from the Police Academy.

"We're ensuring that we permit everyone in New York City that needs to apply and have the chance to work in the best police division in the country, to ensure we give them that open door," the official said.

Gatherings speaking to Sikh and Muslim officers inside the office said individuals who were beforehand conceded religious facilities are as of now permitted to exploit the modified arrangements, which are required to be finished one month from now. The Muslim Officers Society and the more up to date Sikh Officers Association, which have more than 1,100 individuals joined, had been pushing for the progressions.

The accommodation are required to give help to officers whose religious articulations conflicted with those from the Police Department. For Sikhs, complying with the benchmarks in the watch direct has implied shaving the beards their confidence requires to keep uncut, and stuffing their unshorn hair into turbans that fit under office issued tops.

Officer Gurvinder Singh, the leader of the Sikh Officers Association, which has around 150 individuals, said the change would help the division's endeavors to select a more assorted compel. He anticipated that more Sikh applicants would join to take the police exam in January, refering to telephone calls he had gotten from religious and community pioneers after the declaration.

"A considerable measure of their children needed to join, yet they wouldn't," he be able to said. "Furthermore, now they can. This nation has given us a considerable measure, and now we need to pay it back."

Mr. O'Neill declared the reconsidered approaches at Madison Square Garden, where 557 volunteers moved on from the Police

Academy. Thirty-three of those graduates are Muslims and two are Sikhs, as indicated by the Police Department.

In the fall, the Police Department conceded two Sikh enlisted people religious facilities that enabled them to develop beards reaching out up to a large portion of an inch from their countenances while at the academy, as indicated by the Sikh Coalition, a Sikh social equality Association which speaks to one of the officers. Their customer did not ask for or get a settlement for the turban, as per the coalition's lawful executive, Harsimran Kaur, who extolled the updates.

"The N.Y.P.D's. refusal to enlist turbaned and whiskery Sikhs enables different managers to justify declining to enlist Sikhs," she said. "If the N.Y.P.D's. new approach in reality considers Sikhs to keep up unshorn beards and turbans, that sends a solid message that Sikhs are a piece of the standard texture of America."

Prabhden Singh, 6, his hair wrapped in an indigo turban, skipped around outside the Gurdwara Sikh Cultural Society working in Richmond Hill, Queens. His dad, Jagjeet Singh, 32, a black turban over his hair and thick whiskers covering his button, said the office's approach change was "an incredible thing" for the Sikh community.

Mr. Singh, who drives a taxi, said individuals regularly asked in regards to his turban and his legacy — many inquired as to whether he was Muslim. "I get a kick out of the chance to clarify my identity, and where we are from," he stated, including that he appreciated clarifying the historical backdrop of the turban to those new to the way of life.

Also, the approach change, Mr. Singh stated, will make an open door for individuals to get some information about their Sikh legacy also. A great many people, he included, basically don't know much about the Sikh culture.

CHAPTER EIGHT

DIVERSITY IN LAW ENFORCEMENT POTENTIALLY STRENGTHENS COMMUNITY TRUST

Disastrous occasions in recent years - including officer-included shootings and assaults on law enforcement officers, and the shows and dissents these episodes have generated - have caught people in general's consideration and driven a large group of policing issues from the outskirts to the focal point of our open discourse, including a restored concentrate on expanding diversity in the country's law enforcement organizations. In December 2014, President Obama declared his Task Force on 21st Century Policing (Task Force). The Task Force united a various scope of partners - including law enforcement pioneers, advocates, scholastics, policymakers, and community individuals - to investigate systems for reinforcing community-police relations, decreasing wrongdoing, and propelling open security. In one of its key proposals for "building trust and legitimacy" in community-police relations, the Task Force concentrated on the need to guarantee law enforcement offices better mirror the diversity of the groups they serve.

In spite of the fact that the focus on these issues may appear to be new to few, for some - including law enforcement faculty, government authorities, and community pioneers - this is just a single piece of a decades-in length discussion about how law enforcement and the groups they serve can best cooperate. Numerous law enforcement offices, and in addition associations that work with law enforcement, have given significant time, energy, and consideration in their endeavors to enroll and hold workforces that mirror the diversity inside their purviews. For a long time, the Federal government has likewise attempted to deliver difficulties and hindrances to diversity in law enforcement.

Advancing Diversity in Law Enforcement Initiative

The U.S. Division of Justice and the U.S. Equal Employment Opportunity Commission keep on leading hearty enforcement, information investigation, and specialized help endeavors to address diversity in law enforcement. However, these endeavors, without anyone else, can't achieve the greater part of the more than 18,000 law enforcement offices in the nation. In reality, intentional endeavors by law enforcement bosses are a similarly, if not progressively, critical approach to propel diversity and further equivalent work opportunity. Toward that end, in December 2015, the Department's Civil Rights Division and the EEOC propelled another exploration activity, "Propelling Diversity in Law Enforcement," both to identify hindrances that undermine diversity in law enforcement and to feature promising practices that assistance organizations better mirror the diversity of the groups they serve. The activity has concentrated on hindrances and promising practices crosswise over three key zones: enlistment, contracting, and maintenance. In this manner, this activity has taken a wide examination of different obstructions to diversity, while likewise setting specific accentuation on hones that progress more prominent racial and sexual orientation diversity and that encourage the incorporation of the points of view and encounters of people of various foundations in the way of life and administration of law enforcement organizations. This activity was made to help law enforcement offices all through the nation as they endeavor to assemble workforces that better mirror the diversity of the groups they serve. The expectation this exertion will particularly help those little and medium-estimate police divisions that perceive the significance of diversity, yet may do not have the assets to completely investigate arrangements.

Why Diversity in Law Enforcement Matters

The test of enlisting, procuring, and holding a various workforce is absolutely not restricted to law enforcement. All through the nation, in about each part of society, individuals and associations are thinking about this issue. Businesses in an assortment of ventures have occupied with proactive endeavors to reinforce diversity. However, this test remains especially pressing in the field of law enforcement. Law enforcement offices satisfy a key part in our general public, and in numerous groups, singular police officers are regularly the general population face of nearby government. It in this way is important that our country's law enforcement organizations extensively mirror the diversity of the groups they serve.

As the Task Force perceived, expanded diversity inside law enforcement offices - characterized regarding race and sex, as well as different qualities including religion, sexual introduction, sex personality, dialect capacity, foundation, and experience - fills in as a basically essential apparatus to manufacture trust with groups. This finding is reinforced by many years of research affirming that when individuals from general society trust their law enforcement associations speak to them, comprehend them, and react to them - and when groups see experts as reasonable, genuine, and responsible - it develops trust in law enforcement, imparts open trust in government, and backings the uprightness of majority rules system. This trust is basic to defusing pressure, to unraveling wrongdoings, and to making a framework in which occupants see law enforcement as reasonable and just. Casualties and observers of wrongdoing may not approach or draw in with law enforcement if they don't see such specialists to be receptive to their encounters and concerns. This trust - and the participation it encourages - additionally empowers officers to all the more successfully and securely play out their duties.

Research additionally recommends that expanded diversity can make law enforcement organizations more open to change, all the more ready to start social and systemic changes, and more receptive to the inhabitants they serve. Some have indicated expanded diversity as an impetus for change, empowering officers and law enforcement pioneers alike to wind up plainly more contemplative and intelligent about issues in their areas of expertise. A more intelligent and liberal culture in an office can enable drive to change over a scope of regions, including non military personnel oversight, community policing, and racial inclination. Also, while more prominent workforce diversity alone can't guarantee reasonable and compelling policing, a significant - and developing - body of proof proposes that diversity can impact specific exercises and practices of law enforcement organizations.

Hindrances to Diversity

Regardless of their endeavors, law enforcement offices of all sizes have not generally been effective in enrolling and pulling in people that mirrors the groups they serve. This is likely inferable from various elements that are available in the enrolling, hiring, and maintenance stages.

Recruitment:

Stressed relations and an absence of trust of law enforcement may dissuade people from underrepresented groups from applying to be officers.

The notoriety or operational practices of law enforcement offices may prevent candidates from underrepresented groups from seeking after a vocation in law enforcement.

People from underrepresented groups may not be adequately mindful of vocation benefits inside law enforcement offices.

Hiring:

Law enforcement offices' dependence on insufficiently custom-made examinations as a major aspect of the screening procedure may have the unintended result of barring qualified people in underrepresented groups from the candidate pool.

Dependence on certain extra choice criteria and screening forms that excessively affects people from underrepresented groups can likewise hinder organizations' endeavors to expand the diversity of their workforces.

Necessities, for example, residency confinements, may restrict certain underrepresented groups' portrayal in law enforcement offices.

Length, multifaceted nature and cost of use procedures can fill in as an obstruction for candidates.

Law enforcement organizations might be restricted in their capacity to modify or alter hiring and determination criteria.

Retension:

People may confront difficulties acclimating to a law enforcement office's hierarchical culture.

People from underrepresented groups may confront difficulties in the advancement procedure because of an absence of straightforwardness about the procedure, and also a shortage of good examples, tutoring connections, and expert improvement openings.

In identifying arrangements and practices that have filled in as boundaries to enlisting, hiring, and holding a workforce that mirrors the diversity of the community, this report is not proposing that law enforcement organizations ought to fundamentally forsake those approaches or practices. Truth be told, some of these approaches and practices result from prerequisites of government, state, as well as nearby laws. Be that as it may, to the degree offices are attempting to build the diversity of their workforces, they have to perceive that these boundaries may block their capacity to do as such and create procedures to adjust for the hindrances' undesired effect.

Promising Practices for Increasing Diversity

By embracing proactive and purposeful recruitment, hiring, and maintenance techniques, law enforcement offices can address obstructions, drive change, and gain ground in guaranteeing that their workforces better mirror the diversity of the groups they serve. The report features promising practices - identified through existing on the web materials, autonomous research, and meetings - that different law enforcement offices have observed to be especially powerful at expanding their diversity. Given the sheer number of law enforcement offices in this nation, this report does not give a far reaching examination of promising practices that have been produced and are being utilized, yet it provides various striking cases concentrated on the key ranges of (i) recruitment, (ii) hiring, and (iii) maintenance. Despite the fact that the practices received by law enforcement offices shift extensively, this report shows that effective diversity-building endeavors by law enforcement offices share few basic topics, including:

Guaranteeing that the office's authoritative culture is guided by community policing (a technique of policing that spotlights on police building ties and working intimately with community individuals); procedural equity (the possibility of decency in the procedures that settle debate) and social inclusivity (inviting and including all individuals).

Drawing in partners both from inside and outside the law enforcement office - to help make a workforce that mirrors the diversity of the community.

Being ready to re-assess business criteria, principles, and benchmarks to guarantee that they are custom fitted to the skills expected to perform work capacities, and therefore pull in, select, and hold the most qualified and alluring sworn officers.

Recruitment:

Proactive and focused on community outreach endeavors can help support individuals from different populaces and strolls of life to consider vocations in law enforcement.

Building associations with instructive establishments and giving youngsters entry level position programs makes a hearty pipeline of potential candidates while likewise tending to verifiably negative recognitions or encounters assorted groups have had with law enforcement.

The compelling, inventive utilization of innovation and online networking is basic to impart and associate with all individuals from the community.

Hiring:

Offices are progressively receiving an all encompassing perspective of what skills and qualities a candidate conveys to a law enforcement office, to a limited extent by being willing to reexamine data uncovered amid individual verifications, including past medication utilize.

Law enforcement organizations have communicated an eagerness to re-examine determination criteria and composed or physical examinations that don't compare to work related obligations, and that lopsidedly screen out people from underrepresented populaces.

In their endeavors to diversify their workforces, law enforcement offices have streamlined and made more straightforward their hiring and determination systems. A few organizations have offered help and planning materials to enable candidates to get ready for examinations.

Law enforcement offices have included community individuals in the hiring procedure as an approach to create workforces that mirrors the diversity of their groups.

Retention:

Mentorship projects and initiative preparing are basic to giving new officers - especially those from underrepresented populaces - with the help, direction, and assets they have to prevail at work, make the most of their vocations, and gain advancements.

Community organizations and partner engagement can help hold officers of color and ladies by better understanding the one of a kind difficulties they confront in the calling.

Impetuses - including giving impermanent lodging, enabling officers to work towards school credit while at work, and giving budgetary rewards to language skills - can assist hold officers with assorted encounters and foundations.

Law enforcement organizations that are focused on expanding the diversity of their workforces and guaranteeing that the demographic settings of their sworn officers mirror the diversity of the groups they serve confront a plenty of difficulties. These difficulties, which manifest themselves at each phase of the recruitment, choice, and maintenance forms, are overwhelming, however - as the encounters of the law enforcement offices featured in this report clarify - they are a long way from unrealistic. Truth be told, organizations that have attempted this exertion have discovered that expanded diversity brings a scope of advantages that can be seen both inside their workforces and in their relations with the groups they serve. The expectation this current report's talk of hindrances that restrain diversity and the promising practices that have been received and are being utilized as a part of wards the whole way across the nation give a helpful asset to law enforcement organizations, especially those that might not have the inward assets to embrace this kind of survey themselves.

In the meantime, the work accomplished for the Advancing Diversity in Law Enforcement activity has uncovered various unanswered inquiries and regions for future research and survey. Specifically:

More work should be done to comprehend the effect of expanded workforce diversity on the enforcement exercises of law enforcement offices.

Extra exact research is needed to better comprehend the long haul effects of the promising practices featured in this report.

Additionally, research could break down how to additionally organize these promising practices inside offices so they can withstand changes in initiative and faculty.

At the point when government partners and policymakers consider laws and directions that effect determination techniques and criteria for law enforcement offices, the effects on the offices' capacity to employ officers that mirror the diversity of their groups ought to be considered.

Additionally examine is expected to better see how law enforcement offices can effectively hold and cultivate professional success of officers from underrepresented populaces.

This report does not speak to the end of the U.S. Bureau of Justice's Civil Rights Division and the EEOC's work around these imperative issues. The Federal government stays focused on collaborating with law enforcement organizations from the whole way across the nation to help them in their endeavors to better mirror the diversity of the groups they serve.

Stressing diversity in law enforcement

As the nation commemorates the 50th anniversary of the historic March on Washington, I would like to share a few thoughts about why diversity is so vital to the success of law enforcement agencies nationwide.

But there was an African-American sergeant in our neighborhood who took me under his wing and encouraged me to consider a career in law enforcement. We trusted him, and he knew how essential it was to build trust in the people and community he served. He was able to do it better than most, because he looked like us, cared about us, and understood our community.

The law enforcement profession has advanced to new heights, but our best resources are our people in uniform and the people in our communities. Our communities today are more diverse than my neighborhood in Brooklyn. Having racially and ethnically diverse officers allows us to make meaningful connections to the people we serve.

I know from my experiences as a law enforcement leader that when people trust us, they are more likely to report quality-of-life issues, assist in informal crime prevention measures, and have a higher amount of respect for us and the work we do. This respect leads to greater safety for law enforcement officers and enables us to be more effective in preventing crime.

I often speak to fellow law enforcement officers about three key ways to build the kind of diversity that supports public safety.

1) Look to higher education institutions for top talent. That means actively recruiting young men and women from historically black colleges. This enables law enforcement agencies to bring in well-educated officers who are able to establish a greater sense of trust with the community.

2) Recognize the power of young minds and focus on youth development. Law enforcement agencies should support opportunities to connect with children. This helps break through the negative stigma often associated with a career in law enforcement.

Through the Newport News Sheriff's Office Law Enforcement Explorer program, we're able to go into schools to talk with kids in small groups. The conversations can be amazing – we always feel like we've made progress in establishing rapport and trust. We must show at-risk kids that they have the power to dream and achieve greatness.

We also work with the students in the An Achievable Dream schools. When the kids graduate, they say, "Look at me, I'm a dreamer!" They know they can count on us as part of their support system.

3) Help at-risk youth get on track for successful lives. Children living in poverty face so many difficulties that greatly inhibit their ability to grow into the kind of representatives we need. Investing in high-quality preschool will give more kids a foundation for academic success. As police officers, we must show America that our job is not just about locking people up. Keeping our communities safe starts very early on, by investing in our children.

These ideas enable all citizens to realize a great deal more of the dream articulated 50 years ago today: greater harmony in our diverse communities, and greater public safety for all.

CHAPTER NINE

SOME CHALLENGES IN HEALING THE DIVIDE

The shooting of an unarmed black young person by a white cop in Ferguson, Missouri, has propelled across the country challenge and reflection about (in addition to other things) the racial elements of police offices and the communities they serve.

A stark measurement—while the community of Ferguson is 66% black, the police division is 94 percent white—has been refered to far and wide in news scope and investigation. So have the actualities that 86 percent of movement stops there are endured by black drivers, as are 93 percent of the subsequent captures.

Clearly such a divergence in the racial make-up amongst police and policed could prompt a us-versus-them attitude that is useless, and at last hazardous. So head of police and government officials the nation over are on the whole contemplating how they can attempt to cure the awkwardness.

"Notwithstanding WHO IS CARRYING OUT THE POLICE FUNCTION, POLICE WILL ALWAYS BE SEEN AS REPRESENTATIVES OF THE LARGER ESTABLISHMENT. All things considered, TENSIONS BETWEEN POLICE AND CITIZENS MAY BE A FUNCTION OF THE POLICE ROLE."

Lawyer General Eric Holder discharged an announcement a week ago saying that Ferguson "ought to consider the part that expanded diversity in law enforcement can play in building trust inside groups." Thomas Wydra, police head of Hamden, Connecticut, says he's attempting to expand diversity in his positions since, when police officers "resemble" the general population in the community where they work, "that gives the division legitimacy." Des Moines, Iowa's Police Sergeant Jason Halifax says he and his partners are "frustrated" with the absence of diversity in his specialty, however discloses that their endeavors to enroll minorities simply aren't working.

Back in Ferguson, comparable cases are made. Chairman James Knowles III told columnists that the issue is an absence of enthusiasm among youthful black occupants. The office would enlist minorities if they connected, yet "they as of now have this distinction with law enforcement." Meanwhile, the issue compounds and strengthens itself with each new era. "The discernment is that if we don't have the diversity, we don't have the comprehension," Ferguson Police Chief Jackson disclosed to theWall Street Journal. "Also, recognition is reality."

Tracie Keesee, fellow benefactor of the Center for Policing Equity at the University of California-Los Angeles, made the rounds on PBS and NPR a week ago to discuss the gigantic obstacle that the chronicled connection between police divisions and groups of shading can be to recruitment. (The Center for Policing Equity, unexpectedly, happened to target close-by St. Louis this past May for an investigation on racial diversity and racial profiling inside its police compel.)

Keesee herself is an African-American lady, and a 25-year veteran of the Denver Police Department, now a skipper. At the point when Keesee disclosed to her mom, who experienced childhood in the South amid the Civil Rights development, that she needed to join the constrain, her mom's response was one of profound worry for her security. In any case, she stated, that profoundly imbued memorable racial irregularity can't be turned around just through governmental policy regarding minorities in society in police enrolling endeavors. Divisions that endeavor to rapidly diversify may confront new entanglements.

Diversity "helps mentally, and it helps from now and then a correspondences outlook," Keesee revealed to Melissa Block on

NPR's All Things Considered. "Be that as it may, a great deal of times, if you have somebody that is not set up to carry out that occupation, there's likewise an inclination for overcompensation ... you have people that can mirror the community that on occasion happen to be significantly more vicious than the bigger gathering that most people are furious at."

There's no real way to know whether a more different compel could have kept the heightening of pressure in Ferguson, or whatever other circumstances like it, Keesee said; "it isn't so much that basic."

Research by criminologists in the past has also dismisses oversimplified answers for police brutality and racial pressure. In an investigation of 186 "officer-included shootings" in Riverside County, California, analysts composing for the diary Criminal Justice and Behaviorfound that white officers will probably shoot than non-white officers, yet a past investigation of police shootings in Chicago for the Journal of Criminal Law and Criminology found that black officers will probably shoot than white officers. The examinations were of different spots and different circumstances, so it's difficult to sum up from them.

Brad W. Smith, a specialist from Wayne State University, set out to evaluate the immediate effect of the diversity of divisions on police-caused crimes. A difficult errand, certainly. His examination, distributed in the Policy Studies Journalin 2003, found that, while the racial make-up of a community measurably affected the commonness of police savagery there (specifically, the bigger the black populace, the more continuous the viciousness), the extent of minority police officers to white police officers in a division "had no significant impact on levels of police brutality."

Smith bets, a figure with respect to why this might be. "The least difficult clarification is that expanded racial diversity in substantial metropolitan police organizations may have no relationship to police-national relations and along these lines police killings," he composes. "Notwithstanding who is completing the police work, police will dependably be viewed as agents of the bigger foundation. In that capacity, strains amongst police and nationals might be an element of the police part."

At the end of the day, the color of the uniform might be more significant than the color of the skin. What's more, expanding diversity in police offices—while a smart thought for upgrading long haul trust—is no simple fix for the profound situated strain amongst police and the policed, and the heartbreaking brutality that occasionally emits subsequently.

Identified barriers

One of the issues that can enormously affect (trust) is whether law enforcement organizations mirror the communities they serve, whether they resemble the communities they serve," Deputy Attorney General Sally Q. Yates said Wednesday in declaring the report's discharge.

The report refers to a 2013 study from the Justice Department's Bureau of Justice Statistics demonstrating that racial or ethnic minorities make up around 27 percent of full-time sworn officers in the more than 12,000 nearby police offices the nation over. That rate, however higher than it was 30 years prior, still implies that minorities are underrepresented in law enforcement in numerous communities, the report said. And keeping in mind that the absence of diversity is particularly intense in residential area police offices, the issue is not restricted to those offices, authorities say.

"Our own government offices, our own particular DOJ offices, are not so different as they could be," Yates stated, reverberating comments from FBI Director James Comey, who has depicted the absence of diversity in his own office as an "emergency."

The report recognizes that minorities might be deflected from joining their police strengths as a result of stressed relations, an absence of trust in law enforcement, an application procedure that screens out people who may somehow be qualified —, for example, through credit checks or inquiries concerning past drug — and an advancement procedure that can put minorities off guard.

The report applauds the police in Richmond, California, for catching up with candidates when a drug issue emerges instead of consequently disqualifying them. It additionally singles out the police office in Beaufort, South Carolina, for making associations with nearby academy and military foundations and in addition for hiring an officer from the Dominican Republic and paying for English classes to enable him to enhance his language skills.

Not an easy job but opportunities to be better exist

One of the best things about my job is the opportunity to get to know the leadership of American law enforcement. Over the last three years, I have had the good fortune to know and talk with many of you. And although I haven't walked in your shoes, I thought it might be useful to share a perspective from where I am, as part of an organization that is in all of your communities, depends upon you, and constantly learns from you.

I have learned from you that this is a uniquely difficult time in American law enforcement. I realize that "unique" is an overused word, but I think it applies here. And enough of you have told me that this is the hardest time in your career that I suspect you agree.

Your people are caught in difficult and dangerous riptides. Your patrol officers, your deputies, your detectives, your agents face challenges that those who came before them could hardly imagine.

There is water rushing in and water rushing out, and your people are standing where these unpredictable currents meet. They are being pulled in different directions. They are being pulled by the communities they serve, by their colleagues, by expectations, by their leaders, by the media.

There is a very real chance of drowning in the currents.

There is a need for leadership in the middle of those riptides. There is a need for people to stand tall, plant their feet, speak the truth, and calm the waters.

So what kind of leaders are we looking for standing like that among the riptides?

First of all, they are leaders who know their people. They know they became cops and sheriffs to do good. To help others. To serve their communities and to serve all the people who live there—whatever race, nationality, religion, gender, sexual orientation they may be. Your folks signed up to serve all of the people, all of the time.

Second, the leaders we need know what good policing looks like. They know it because they have lived it. Up-close, respectful, disciplined, firm, fair, lawful, and transparent law enforcement is what has always worked best, even in neighborhoods with the most significant crime problems. The leaders we need understand that a combination of kindness and toughness, of humility and confidence, of decency and determination, delivers the best results.

Third, the leaders we need know their neighborhoods with the greatest need for police and they know the people who live there. In particular, they know the history and journey of black America. They know the hopes, the dreams, the disappointments and the pain. They know the history of law enforcement's interaction with black America, because the black people of America know it and remember it for reasons that make good sense. They know that African-Americans, like all Americans, want good policing because they know it is the path to safety and prosperity.

Fourth, the leaders we need understand that our challenges are multiplied by a narrative that is forming about American policing. It is a narrative that has formed, in the absence of good information and in the absence of actual data, and it is this: Biased police are killing black men at epidemic rates. That is the narrative. It is a narrative driven by video images of real misconduct, possible misconduct, and perceived misconduct. It is a narrative given force by the power of empathy. It is also a narrative pushed forward by the surprise and shock of civilians at seeing how fast and complicated police activity can be.

The leaders we need know that many people of good will in this country—decent, caring people—believe with all their hearts that American law enforcement is using deadly force against black people at epidemic levels. The leaders we need know Americans believe that because those are the videos they see, over and over and over again. To these Americans, people of good will and good hearts, each video becomes further proof of nationwide police brutality. People of good will are protesting—including here in San Diego—because they believe there is an epidemic of police violence against black people.

Of course, however good their hearts, however good their intentions, Americans actually have no idea whether the number of black people or brown people or white people being shot by police is up, down, or sideways over the last 10 years. They have no idea whether black people or brown people are more likely to be shot during encounters than white people are. There is actually some recent research from a Harvard economist who focused on 10 major departments, analyzing over 1,000 shootings showing lethal force is more likely to be used against white people, while non-lethal force is more likely to be used against black people. But we really don't know well enough on a national basis.

There were 10.7 million arrests in this country last year, and many times that number of encounters between officers and civilians. Out of those tens of millions of encounters, how many people were shot? What did they look like? What were the circumstances? Is deadly force use trending up or down? Where is it worst and where is it best? Nobody knows.

They have no idea of these things because we have no idea of these things. We simply don't know. As a country, we simply haven't bothered to collect the data, to gather the information.

And in the absence of information, we have anecdotes, we have videos, we have good people believing something terrible is going on. In a nation of almost a million law enforcement officers and tens of millions of police encounters each year, a small group of videos serve as proof of an epidemic.

The leaders we need know that this narrative makes it hard to gain our footing. It makes it hard for us to help people. Because in the absence of information, the narrative dominates and it changes everything. The leaders we need know we simply must change that and show ourselves and America what is true and accurate. Whatever that may be. We must have a national database about our use of deadly force. With accurate information, we can all get better.

The leaders we need also know that the narrative divides us, that it can keep good officers in their cars and good people in their homes, separated by a chasm of fear and distrust.

The leaders we need know that our officers are human beings, with families, obligations, hopes, and dreams. They know our officers do not want to get famous or get dead. Our officers see the videos. They desperately do not want to be in one. They think about it all the time.

They also saw Dallas and Baton Rouge and Palm Springs and they follow every end-of-watch notification. They think about that all the time. They desperately don't want to leave their family behind, and their families desperately don't want to be left behind.

The leaders we need worry that self-initiated police activity is on the decline in our most violent cities. Of course officers respond to calls; of course they make arrests, comfort victims, and interview witnesses. They still "do their jobs." They still risk their lives. Because they are good people. But they are also people and a good leader knows that.

The leaders we need ask questions: Do my officers get out of their car at midnight to ask a group of kids what their business is on a street corner? Do they stop the car with tinted windows that just ran a stop sign in a high-crime neighborhood? Do they get out to pat down the known offender who has been standing for an hour on a known drug corner? Or, as you have told me, do they first ask themselves, "Could this get me famous or dead?" And the answer changes policing and changes neighborhoods. The leaders we need see that.

But they also see that's only one side of the divide. On the other side of the divide, the chasm of distrust, they know stand good people who saw something, or suspect something, or know something. When homicides are up but clearance rates are down, the leaders we need think about the divide, the chasm. If people don't trust the police, they aren't going to offer the tips, they aren't going to whisper to the cop that they saw the up-close shooting, that they know who just left 20 shell casings on the sidewalk in broad daylight, that they know where the gun ended up. Instead, they are going to stay inside on their own side of the divide, the chasm. More murders, more unsolved.

And so into the chasm, into the gap of distrust, fall more dead young black men. Places like Chicago show us what the chasm looks like and how much pain it causes. The leaders we need ache over this, agonize over this, and refuse to stop speaking about it.

And so they keep talking, until they are hoarse. They talk to their citizens. They talk to the media. They talk to their local elected leaders. And, most of all, they talk to their officers. They love them and support them and hold them accountable. They fight for the equipment and training they need. They make clear what is expected of them, and make clear that they will have their back if they police well, even if it ends badly, even if it ends in tragedy, as it sometimes does.

And to their communities, they make clear that good policing is up-close and firm-but-respectful; that policing is really, really hard and sometimes bad things happen, but those things will be met with transparency and sound judgment; that community leaders should support their officers because they are, after all, their officers, saving lives and creating spaces where good things can grow.

And in all that talking, the leaders we need show both sides they want and need the same policing. That is how the chasm will begin to close. That is how communities will find both healing and peace.

Those are the kind of leaders we need. The good news? Those are the kind of leaders so many of our communities have. I have come to know many of you personally as I have met with you and your troops, so I know we have these kinds of leaders, all across the country. Leaders who are planting your feet in the riptide, caring for your officers and for your community, and for helping calm the waters. Thank you for being those leaders. We need you now more than ever.

But as you work to close the chasm, we face another threat from the narrative that policing is biased and violent and unfair. It threatens the future of policing, so we have to talk about it as well.

Who would chose to do this work? Who would choose to do something decried as inherently racist? Who would choose to risk getting famous or dead? Why on earth would a talented young person choose that life when they could choose a "respectable" profession?

These questions should haunt us as law enforcement leaders, because this country will be deeply sorry if that young talent—kids who want to help others—chooses some other way to serve. We need great teachers, and nurses, and social workers. But we also need great people of character and talent out there where the stakes are highest—where single moms are trying to find a life for their families, where a good kid needs a second chance, where old people want to sit on the porch, where there really are predators trying to kill people.

We need talent there.

If quality young people stop signing up, we may not notice it for a few years, but the day will come when we will be deeply sorry that we failed to explain to great young people why they should choose law enforcement, that we failed to show them the true heart of law enforcement.

There are bad cops. There are departments with troubled cultures. Unfortunately, people are flawed. In any large group, there will be bad ones. All professions want to find and root out the bad ones. There are bad bankers, bad lawyers, and bad software engineers. There are companies and firms with troubled cultures. But for law enforcement, the spotlight is brighter and the standards are higher. That is the way it should be, given the power and authority we are entrusted with. We accept those standards and must work hard to measure ourselves against them.

And of course the pressure on cops is unique. There is no doubt that some cops come to see young men of color on their beat as perps because they see so many who have gone wrong. That's dumb and unjust and we have to constantly resist it, to train it out and root it out.

Cops are also only called to scenes of hurt and pain; that can be warping and we have to be conscious of that danger. We have to show the cops who only work the overnight that there are good people in that neighborhood going to school and work, pushing strollers, and sitting on park benches in the daylight, including good young men trying to make a life.

But I really can't give you an on-the-one-hand, on-the-other-hand thing here, because the truth is this: Police officers are overwhelmingly good people. They are overwhelmingly people who took exhausting, dangerous jobs because they want to help people. They chose lives of service over self, lives of moral content, because that's who they are. They want to stop bad guys from occupying neighborhoods; they want to help old people off the floor and back into bed; they want to keep a young girl from a life on the street.

Someone once said that you make a living by what you get; you make a life by what you give. These cops don't make a great living. But they make a great life, for themselves, and for those they protect.

As we work to close the chasm, we need to show the young people of America what it is like to choose service over self. We need to show them what American law enforcement is really like.

Because if they know what we know, they will want to be part of it. And we also need to show the people of America, especially people of color and especially the black community, what we are really like. Because if they see what we see, the chasm will start to close.

I saw the true heart of American law enforcement in a church in Orlando in June. I went down to have a private meeting with the first responders to the attack at the Pulse nightclub. I wanted to thank them, in person, and privately.

As I stood looking out at the sea of faces, a hand went up. A man in uniform stood up. He told me his name and then he said, "I'm Jewish." That confused me, but he went on. "I was one of the first there that night, and as I ran toward the sound of gunfire, at my side was a Muslim officer. We were Jew and Muslim and Christian. We were white and black and Latino and Asian. We ran to help people we didn't know and we didn't care what they looked like. We ran toward the danger because that's who we are, that's what we do. I thought you should know that. I think people should know that." And then he sat down.

That is the true heart of law enforcement.

We are flawed. We must—and we will—work to get better. But we are good people from all walks of life who have chosen service over self. I know that. I think all people should know that.

When I speak to young people I try to give them an odd perspective. Because life is filled with striving and stresses, with the need for money and the craving for recognition, all of which may obscure what really matters, I tell them to do something weird. I suggest that they close their eyes and imagine themselves old and gray and about to die. I ask them to sit at the end of their lives and look back on their life and ask one question: "Who do I want to have been?" Because if you ask it that way, things like money and houses and cars and even human honor are stripped away. And what really matters will come into view.

I frame it that way for them because I hope some of them will answer the question as those in law enforcement have. You want to have been people who used what you had to help people who needed you—the bullied, the picked-on, the vulnerable, the weak, the frightened. That's who you will have been. And we must ensure that people of talent continue to understand that only in such a life is there real value, real wealth.

We need to lead well. We need to collect accurate and complete information to inform the policing debates in this country. We need to show people the true heart of law enforcement. And, we need to close the chasm. If we do those things, and we do them well, we will save lives. And we will ensure that other great men and women follow into this frustrating, exhausting, dangerous, and thoroughly wonderful career.

Thank you for your leadership. Thank you for the lives you have chosen to live. Thank you for the lives you shape and the lives you save. Thank you for choosing to do good for a living.

Healing Divisions between Police and the Public

But how do you stop the divisiveness and start healing divisions between the public and law enforcement? How do you build trust while also maintaining order? It is a complex issue. Everyone wants fair and equal treatment without crime and disorder; however, achieving this goal remains elusive.

Every day, politicians talk about the importance of starting a "dialogue." Yes, there needs to be better communication, but there needs to be more than just talking. Both citizens and police want action.

What Do Citizens Want from Police?

People want many things from police, including responding to crimes, preventing crimes, catching criminals, preserving the peace, responding to natural and manmade disasters, assisting homeless people, dealing with the mentally ill and remaining visible in neighborhoods. And that's just a short list of expectations.

As the Dallas police chief said, "We're asking cops to do too much in this country." Police are being asked to take care of many of society's problems, but many citizens don't understand the complexity of being a police officer. Laws, court rulings, community expectations, police training and tactics are constantly changing, which places great stress on individual officers as well as the department.

What Do Police Want from the People?

Many officers consider their job to be a thankless one and do not feel supported by political leaders or community members. But like all those Dallas officers running into the line of fire to protect protesters, police just want to do their job!

When there is a police-involved shooting, cops want what the people want: to be treated fairly and respected. Police want to do their job without being slandered by the media and government leaders. To hear the press state "another person was gunned down by police" makes it sound as if every cop is out gunning for people and it makes most cops sick. To hear politicians comment that the cause of an officer-involved shooting is racism within hours after an incident even when they admit they don't have all the facts is not only promoting racism and hatred, it also fuels the fire for more attacks against police.

Police need citizens' support. An officer loves to hear the words, "Thank you for your service." My reply was always, "Thank you for your support." Stemming back to policing in old England is the premise that "The ability of the police to perform their duties is dependent upon public approval of police actions." Without support, police cannot do what they are sworn to do: protect and serve.

How Do We Talk and Act Together?

A good starting point for community engagement includes participating in organized forums, ride-alongs, enacting community policing strategies and citizen's police academies.

Community Forums

Almost every community has a civic league or some type of forum that meets regularly. These days, there is usually a cop at each meeting. If not, there should be. This is where police can get to know leaders of the community in a non-confrontational way, before there is a problem. If the latter happens, it may be too late to be non-confrontational and the officer is often expected to already know about the problem(s) and be expected to explain what the department is doing about it.

Community Policing Strategies

A Community Oriented Policing (COP) program is not just talking to citizens; it is working hand-in-hand with citizens to identify and solve the problems in their neighborhoods. A main goal of COP is to reduce fear. It may also help calm the anger and starting healing divisions that are often generated by the lack of faith in the criminal justice system.

According to Dr. Leon Seltzer, the move from fear to anger happens at "breathtaking speed." When officers and citizens work together, they can help reduce or remove anxiety and fear before it turns into anger and rage. Police need to work to get citizens more involved so citizens can take responsibility for their own neighborhood — most citizens gladly accept the responsibility. As people get more involved and work closer with police, they often realize and understand some of the dilemmas officers face and how they have to make difficult decisions.

Citizens Police Academy

A citizen's police academy is another good way to introduce citizens to the policing profession. Citizens learn how and why officers are trained to act in the ways they do. Citizens can ask questions, receive immediate answers and learn about particular issues affecting the city and their individual community.

The biggest issue for enacting these community engagement efforts almost always comes down to resources. Most police departments across the U.S. are small and only have a few officers and operate on a limited budget. That is why agencies need to partner with others in nearby jurisdictions, as well as state and federal agencies to share resources. There is also potential to receive grant money. Agencies must realize there are millions of dollars in grant money available to them, but they also can't dismiss the fact that grant writing requires resources as well.

Using Policy to Fix the Problem

Researchers indicate that patrol officers are the "gatekeepers" of the criminal justice system, using their discretion to determine what laws to enforce and what suspects to arrest (Fritsch, Liederbach & Taylor, 2009). It is the role of administrators to limit the amount of discretion an officer can use through established departmental policies. Doing so is no easy task. Department leaders and first-line supervisors must closely monitor officers to ensure they understand and follow policies. When things go wrong, supervisors must assess the situation and take action.

Whenever it is determined the officer was unable to comply with policy, the officer must be trained. If the officer was unwilling to comply, the officer must be disciplined. However, the incident could be the example of a systematic problem. In this case, supervisors need to review and/or revise policies, procedures and training for all officers. When this happens, some officers will resist and test the new policy.

For example, our department enacted a policy prohibiting officers from asking citizens stopped for minor traffic violations if they had guns, drugs and/or large sums of money. The policy was put in place after numerous citizen complaints of being interrogated like criminals. The city and police administrators agreed and implemented a policy that officers should not ask such questions during routine traffic stops, absent reasonable suspicion.

However, one officer decided he was not going to follow the new policy. His supervisor, who often stopped by to assist a lone officer on traffic stops, heard him ask the question to a driver. After the traffic stop, the supervisor asked the officer why he asked the question and the officer said because the Supreme Court said it was okay. The supervisor advised him that the next time he thought about disobeying a policy, to look at his paycheck and see if the payer was the Supreme Court or his police department.

Departments cannot increase police authority beyond the law, but they can certainly restrict it. Some officers may still resist, as every organization has some bad apples, but those bad apples must be retrained or fired. Close supervision of officers is the key to holding the few bad officers accountable.

The Importance of Progressive Hiring in Healing Divisions

There is no doubt that agencies need to hire more minorities. It is widely believed that a police force should be representative of the community it serves. There is evidence that hiring minority officers may have no impact on policing, indicating that neither "race nor gender has an influence on routine police-citizen encounters." However, a diverse force can decrease citizens' fears of being stopped "solely because of race."

Unfortunately, many apply and few are chosen. The hiring process is so rigorous that 80 percent of departments in the U.S. have unfilled positions. The problem with many minorities is they cannot get past the tough application process, which includes a thorough background check, physical, written and physical fitness tests, a polygraph, and, in some departments, a psychological examination like the Behavioral Personnel Assessment Device (BPAD). BPAD is when videos are shown from an officer's point of view featuring various situations with no ending. A police candidate watches the film and pretends to take the place of the officer. For example, a video may show a motorist rolling up his windows and locking his car doors, thereby failing to cooperate on a traffic stop. Those candidates spending the longest time talking to the violator are looked at favorably over those who broke the window and forcefully removed the violator.

The Need to Show Greater Support

Government leaders must show respect and support for the police. Police are, and will continue to serve, as the thin blue line between law and order and anarchy. There has been way too much rhetoric from some of our national and state leaders recently that leaves wrong and even false impressions about police. This rhetoric does nothing to unite our communities, but rather it promotes lawlessness and division. In addition, government leaders must work with police to ensure agencies have the needed resources and training to safely and professionally serve and fulfill their mission.

Citizens also need to show some empathy for the police. Officers don't know what someone else is going to do. They are trained to not only protect others, but to maintain their own safety. Being a police officer is dangerous and unpredictable work.

Officers Also Need to Show Respect for Citizens

Most of the deadly force incidents in the news lately started as minor infractions (e.g. Brown, Garner, and Castile). An officer's approach sets the tone in communicating with the public and healing divisions. At the beginning of my police career, my sergeant gave me the following words of wisdom, "Address everyone as sir or ma'am, and strive to treat everyone you arrest the way you would want your mother to be treated."

First-line supervisors have the most influence on their officers. They must set a good example for the expected behavior of officers. Officers must be culturally aware and guard against "implicit (unintentional) bias." To help with this, progressive departments seek to bring in local officials of minority groups to provide training to officers in the academy as well as during their annual in-service training classes. This dialogue between police and minority leaders can result in both sides reaching a better understanding of the issues and their root causes and healing divisions.

To Be Successful in the Future, We Must Consider the Good Principles of the Past

Overall, there needs to be more respect and understanding from police, citizens, and government officials. One of the Principles of Policing from Sir Robert Peel remains appropriate even today: "The police are citizens and citizens are the police." If everyone makes a greater effort to show support and respect for one another, we can make major strikes to remove the divisiveness and start healing the divisions.

CHAPTER TEN

RECOMMENDATIONS: LESSONS LEARNED & BEST PRACTICES

Today's Law Enforcement Challenges

It is very much perceived that a diverse police force helps construct public trust and, in this way, expands public well-being. In light of the shooting of Michael Brown in Ferguson, Missouri, President Obama delegated a Task Force on 21st Century Policing, under the sponsorship of the U.S. Division of Justice's Office of Community Oriented Policing Services. The Task Force drew together law enforcement, community pioneers, specialists, scholastics and others to look at and suggest "best practices" in policing.

The primary "column" of change suggested by the Task Force was "Building Trust and Legitimacy. As a key method for building this community trust, the Task Force featured the "basic significance of hiring officers who mirror the communities they serve. This Task Force proposal echoes and heaps of research showing how police diversity legitimizes law enforcement specialist, reinforces police strengths, and builds public wellbeing.

The Task Force additionally featured that as police strengths and the communities they serve turn out to be more differing, there is a basic requirement for preparing on "perceiving and standing up to understood predisposition and social responsiveness. Such training ought to be "progressing" and "achieved with the help of support groups that speak to the perspectives of communities that have customarily had ill-disposed associations with law enforcement."

Civil unrest in cities across the country challenges public servants to think analytically about how to restore public confidence and protect citizens from bad actors and events that threaten their safety and security. This article summarizes a four-hour roundtable that DomPrep and the Baltimore Police Department convened to share insights on tactics and approaches for success.

The collaboration of these practitioners is magical in times of testing, disturbances, disasters, and attacks, as well as during a roundtable such as this one. Discussing resource management and sharing lessons learned and best practices are key. Unfortunately, the public did not get a chance to hear the comments and passion that these public servants all possess and exhibit when addressing how to serve the public better and find new ways to outreach within communities.

Rebuilding a Community after Civil Unrest

The death of Trayvon Martin on 26 February 2012 was the beginning of large-scale protests of police nationwide. Five years later, that incident along with the April 2015 death of Freddie Gray and subsequent civil unrest in Baltimore, Maryland, continue to spur law enforcement agencies and community officials to seek ways to bridge public relations gaps. Like other cities affected by protests and civil unrest, the city of Baltimore will never be the same and is striving to effectively address concerns and adapt to a "new normal." City law enforcement officers are careful to ensure that their responses are thoughtful and sensitive and that they engage young people in many ways, including sports and mentoring. However, the delicate balance between public safety and outreach is challenging.

Following the investigation into the Gray case, the Baltimore Police Department received a U.S. Department of Justice decree with a list of requirements, which they now incorporate as standards for their processes, trainings, and technology. Chief Melissa Hyatt, who moderated the roundtable discussion, manages the necessary training for required items in the decree and the underlying concern of how the police department can best relate to the public.

In November 2016, another challenge arose at the Army-Navy Game, when a large protest forced the Baltimore police department to split resources – half dealing with the protest and the other half working the game. That event demonstrated the need to recognize indicators of unrest as they develop in order to mitigate the potential consequences.

The Baltimore Police Department organizes regular sports events for community youth members, movie nights, and school visits. One officer shared how he gives youths plastic police badges to build relationships and awareness within the community. Such efforts ensure that residents engage police officers in roles other than arrests and provide opportunities to begin important conversations. This type of event, especially in problematic communities, helps to build better relationships with residents so that, if something does happen, it will be easier in the backend. In addition, following incidents, the police department sends officers to explain to residents the actions that were taken. Officers regularly visiting schools help to identify problematic students and to build positive relationships with youths.

After the trial of one of the Baltimore police officers in May 2016, the department received word of a large protest (a student walkout) through social media. Instead of dispatching a group of officers, one person (community collaboration officer) was sent to talk to the school via assembly, which was very responsive. One person versus a show of force was better for that group. In response to the fire hose that was cut and resulted in the destruction of a CVS pharmacy during the 2015 unrest, the Baltimore Fire Department recommended that the sentencing be community service rather than jail. Local officials found a person who was apologetic, a leader, and someone they could access to begin to build community trust. A number of officials opposed this recommendation, but one leader held fast to the view that community trust works both ways and was willing to stake his reputation on it. It became a significant breakthrough on all counts.

Challenges & Solutions

Unfortunately, children do not always go home and tell their families what they learn in school or in youth outreach efforts. In addition, community meetings are often not well attended, so it is difficult to measure outreach effectiveness. In the meantime, social media is a common method that community members use during an incident. So, if there is unrest, then the news quickly becomes about the unrest itself rather than about facts and issues. To combat these challenges, Baltimore law enforcement works with churches and seeks to reflect the guardianship role, rather than that of an occupying force. They work to communicate with everyone who is willing to work with them, including critics and even gang members. Some gang members are trusted with actionable information and have facilitated law enforcement messages to their members in ways that the law enforcement community alone could not have done.

The February roundtable highlighted that many agencies are available to collaborate and coordinate with local law enforcement. For example, DHS protective security advisors bring together the public and private sectors to educate and empower them to know what to do and how to coordinate a multiagency community. The underlying theme of the discussion was that showing respect increases the chance of receiving respect. Since it is almost impossible to control messages once they hit social media, the human element becomes critical. When community members know the people managing the issues, it changes the dynamics. This would be a good lesson to teach in police academies.

Other best practices include using de-escalation techniques to promote more positive outcomes and develop viable relationships before incidents occur to instill trust and move toward more positive resolutions. Police in Baltimore are extending that respect first. Some of the people involved in the protestors' actions did not see the officers as humans, but instead as game-like "storm troopers," thus distorting the real consequences of their actions.

In addition to building community relationships before an incident, each officer plays a critical role during an incident. As such, Officers and their agencies have responsibility for the responders' safety and well being throughout the incident. For example, when managing an effective response, officers need to be rested and have replacements available who also are ready to come in rested, fed, and hydrated.

Media wants to be engaged with facts and should be used more in time of crisis and potentially during planning, training, and exercises. When no or little information is provided from agency sources, the gaps may be filled with false information. For example, in 2015, following the unrest in Baltimore, a national news reporter inaccurately stated that a man was shot in the back by police. The news anchor issued an apology the following Monday for the erroneous report. The Baltimore Police Department quickly spoke with community members on the scene of the incident, including gang members, to dispel such rumors.

Officials indicated that they are seeing more sharing of knowledge and resources and it seems to be working well across the nation. For example, the 217th Legislature of New Jersey has emphasized information sharing and created a bill in 2016 that established the "New Jersey Criminal Justice Information Sharing Environment Coordinating Council" in the Division of State Police in the Department of Law and Public Safety. Emergency management also falls under New Jersey's (and Michigan's) state police:

The duty of this 15-member council is to establish a governance structure to guide the design, development, and implementation of a Statewide, integrated criminal justice environment that would enable automated information sharing in a common format between federal, State, county, and municipal criminal justice agencies.

Roundtable participants estimated that it will take a year or two for the various stakeholders in Baltimore to get past egos and go beyond these issues, but they are making great strides to collectively tackle problems.

Technological Assets & Lessons Learned

In today's world, where incidents on video are viewed as factual, some roundtable participants worried that a time may come when events not captured on camera will not be considered true. Technology including body-worn cameras have been tested in Baltimore and are being fully implemented. However, questions remain about the recordings, access to them, use of them in court, etc. For example, participants questioned whether officers should be able to review the film to help trigger their memories because sometimes events happen so quickly, so they may not recall specific details.

The use of biometrics is also expanding rapidly across the country. One example is recognition technology, which is moving to standoff distances, but is still able to validate that people are who they say they are. Smart Cities advises being aware of what communities are investing in, and how these investments can be leveraged. Growing technological trends include mobile capabilities and Wi-Fi access points, which may manifest as kiosks and increase interaction between first responders, social workers, mental health professionals, and others. Smart Cities, such as Santa Cruz, California, are considering an alternative use of smart-city technology. Santa Cruz, where local authorities analyze historical crime data in order to predict police requirements and maximize police presence where it is required, generated a list of 10 places each day where property crimes are more likely to occur and then place police efforts there when they are not responding to other emergencies. This use of information and communication technology is different to the manner used outside the United States.

As law enforcement agencies continue to move forward, many aspects in law enforcement will continue to change. Technological advances dictate the need for new computers, radios, software programs, and other related equipment. Society demands a different response from law enforcement than it required during the 1960s. Agencies must focus on image management, public relations, and the impression that appearance and actions make on the general public.

To accomplish the task of bridging public relation gaps, modern law enforcement agencies must be flexible and have adaptable leaders. Those who are still committed to "doing it like we've always done it" are rapidly becoming dinosaurs in a constantly evolving profession. The same is true for those managing civil unrest or protests. This new environment requires flexible and forward-thinking people to continue to transform with the times.

All points made during the roundtable discussion resonate with emergency management and can be summed up as follows:

- Public communications are the key to success in each discipline.
- Innovation in public outreach approaches is necessary.
- Professional sharing of this sort around a high topic raises everyone's frame of reference in a positive manner.
- Building trust is everybody's job and everyone has work to do.

- Partnership is an over-used word, but it is a vital concept in formalizing our outreach in moment-to-moment basis.
- Technology is a driving force and must be used as vigorously by law enforcement agencies as it is by the public. Technology can assist efforts to share actionable information and to accomplish the proper amount of transparency in efforts to build public trust.
- Internal messaging is often as important as external messaging.

When distilling the outcomes and main takeaways, it was apparent that all of the participants at the roundtable discussion are committed to helping their neighborhoods, cities, counties, states, and nation to become resilient and to grow that capability on every level. A future discussion on this topic is warranted in order to review the progress and challenges yet to come.

Special thanks go to the participants of the Baltimore roundtable on 3 February 2017. The dedication of these and other professionals around the country are helping to ensure the effective implementation of whole community action for emergency preparedness, response, and resilience.

Values for Good Policing

The basic role of this distribution is to help law enforcement offices in lessening the occurrence of viciousness between police officers and residents. From the point of view of the police official, the effective achievement of that target ought to have two noteworthy advantages. In the first place, it should improve the well-being of police officers. Second, it should encourage an environment of collaboration and common regard between the police and the general population they serve. The motivation behind this section is to give a premise to evaluating a police office to decide, most importantly, if its way of life is helpful for lessening vicious showdowns between the police and residents. Similarly critical, this section gives a casing of reference which can be utilized by any police boss to create a strategy, decide, execute programs, and, eventually control the way in which the office conveys police administrations to the community.

The Role of Police

The part of policing has been dynamic since it turned into a calling in 1829 under Sir Robert Peel in London, England. The connection amongst police and nationals in American culture is by and large comprehended as a movement from the political time, when police were presented in American urban areas in the 1840s to the mid 1900s; to the change period, extending over the center piece of the twentieth century from the 1930s to the 1970s; and afterward to the community time of current policing since the 1970s.1 Williams and Murphy call attention to the absence of contribution of minorities in policing all through these different times. Communities of shading were to a great extent frail amid the political time and therefore not ready to impact police procedure. Amid the change period, police technique was resolved to a great extent on the premise of law, in spite of the fact that communities of shading were for the most part unprotected.2 In the present community time of policing, one of the principles is the prerequisite for a durable community working in association with a responsive police office. Williams and Murphy express that this precondition does not win in numerous minority neighborhoods.

The Community Relations Service (CRS) of the U.S. Division of Justice has cosponsored various discussions and worked intimately with racial and ethnic police associations, including the Hispanic American Police Command Officers Association, National Asian Peace Officers Association, National Black Police Officers Association, National Latino Peace Officers Association, National Native American Law Enforcement Association, and National Organization of Black Law Enforcement Executives. These discussions concentrated on the connection between minority natives and police. Williams and Murphy accentuate exactly how genuine the exchange about the contemporary part of policing in America is:

The historical backdrop of American police systems can't be isolated from the historical backdrop of the Nation all in all. Lamentably, our police, and the majority of our different organizations, must fight with many sharp heritages from that bigger history. No worldview - and no general public - can be judged tasteful until the point when those inheritances have been gone up against specifically.

The Report of the Independent Commission on the Los Angeles Police Department (July 9, 1991) likewise obtusely states in its foreword that viciousness amongst police and nationals is not something from a period of policing that is behind us:

Police brutality is not a local issue. Perceiving its national character, police boss from 10 note-worthy urban areas met not long after the Rodney King occurrence and stressed that "the issue of unreasonable force in American policing is genuine.

The Police Culture

The "way of life" of a police division reflects what that office has faith in as an association. These convictions are reflected in the office's enlisting and choice practices, arrangements, and systems, preparing and improvement, and at last, in the activities of its officers in law enforcement circumstances. Unmistakably, all police divisions have a culture. The key inquiry is whether that culture has been precisely created or just permitted to create without advantage of thought or direction. There are police organizations, for instance, where police utilization of compel is seen as unusual. Along these lines, when it is utilized, the occasion gets a lot of managerial consideration. Such a reaction mirrors the way of life of that division: the utilization of drive is seen and reacted to as an atypical event. Balance such an office with one which does not see the utilization of drive as anomalous. In the last case, there might be deficient or inadequately comprehended arrangements giving officers rules with respect to the utilization of constraint. There likely is no managerial methodology for researching occurrences where constrain is utilized. Furthermore, in particular, the way of life of the division is with the end goal that officers come to see the utilization of force as a satisfactory method for settling strife.

In the course of recent years, there has been significant advance in enhancing police-community connections. However, the real issue making contact between the police and the community today- - particularly in communities of color - is the police utilization of dangerous force. This is a deep rooted issue of which just lately has people in general end up noticeably mindful. The way that this issue existed for such quite a while before getting across the board consideration can again be identified with the way of life of the police.

Until the Tennessee v. Collect choice in 1985, barely any police divisions had built up their guns arrangement around an esteem framework that reflected respect for human life. Or maybe, those organizations which had composed approaches (and many did not) mirrored the overall police culture in those strategies. The overarching society fixated on enforcement of the law. In this manner, the official strategies of most police organizations enabled officers to discharge cautioning shots, to shoot escaping criminals, or to utilize dangerous compel in different conditions reflected not as much as the most elevated an incentive for human life.

Unmistakably the way of life of a police office, to a substantial degree, decides the association's adequacy. That culture decides the way officers see their part, as well as the general population they serve. The key concern is the idea of that culture and whether it mirrors an arrangement of convictions helpful for the peaceful determination of contention.

How would you set up a positive departmental culture? In noting this inquiry, it is imperative to underscore again that all divisions have a culture. It is additionally imperative to perceive that the way of life of a police office, once settled, is difficult to change. Authoritative change inside a police organization does not happen in a progressive design. Or maybe, it is developmental.

Building up a Set of Values

The starting point in building up a departmental culture is to build up an arrangement of qualities. Qualities fills an arrangement of needs, including:

- Put forward a division's logic of policing

- State in clear terms what an office puts stock in

- Express in expansive terms the general objectives of the office
- Mirror the community's desires of the office
- Fill in as a reason for creating strategies and techniques
- Fill in as the parameters for hierarchical adaptability
- Give the premise to operational methodologies
- Give the system to officer execution
- Fill in as a system from which the office can be assessed

In building up an arrangement of qualities for a police division, it is not important to concoct an extensive rundown. Or maybe, there ought to be a couple of qualities which, when taken together, speak to what the association considers essential. For instance, if it is the target of the office to make a culture that is benefit situated, at that point that ought to be reflected in its arrangement of qualities. At the end of the day, the significance of qualities is subjective, not quantitative.

At last, a basic part of the police boss is to guarantee that the estimations of the division are all around enunciated all through the association. To finish this, the boss as pioneer must guarantee that there is a framework to encourage powerful correspondence of the qualities. This incorporates perceiving and utilizing the association's casual structure. This is critical in light of the fact that, notwithstanding the formal structure, values are transmitted through its casual procedure and additionally its myths, legends, similitudes, and the boss' own identity.

Each police office ought to build up an arrangement of policing esteems that mirrors its own particular community. Luckily, there is a general arrangement of policing esteems that can fill in as a structure for any office to expand upon to address neighborhood issues. Building up an arrangement of hierarchical esteems is not difficult. A police official should first plainly disclose what esteems are to those in uniform. At that point the official ought to solicit every part from the office to list what he or she considers the five most critical esteems for the division. The discoveries of such an activity will speak to an agreement on the qualities division individuals hold most dear- - an astounding beginning stage for making an arrangement of departmental esteems. What takes after is the already said general arrangement of estimations of good policing, which can be the springboard for an office's own detailing:

The police division must safeguard and propel the standards of majority rule government. All social orders must have a framework for looking after request. Police officers in this nation, be that as it may, must know how to look after request, as well as must do as such in a way steady with our popularity based type of government. In this manner, it is occupant upon the police to enforce the law and convey an arrangement of different administrations in a way that jam, as well as expands valuable American esteems. It is in this setting the police turn into the living articulation of the significance and capability of a vote based type of government. The police must regard, as well as ensure the rights ensured to every national by the Constitution. To the degree each officer considers his or her obligation to incorporate insurance of the intrinsically ensured privileges of all people, the police turn into the most critical workers in the huge structure of government.

The police division puts its most elevated an incentive on the protection of human life. Most importantly, the police division must trust that human life is our most valuable asset. In this manner, the division, in all parts of its operations, will put its most astounding need on the assurance of life. This conviction must be manifested in no less than two ways. Initially, the designation of assets and the reaction to requests for benefit must give top need to those circumstances that debilitate life. Second, despite the fact that society approves the police to utilize lethal force, the utilization of such force must be justified under the law, as well as be reliable with the reasoning of balanced and others conscious social control.

The police division trusts that the counteractive action of wrongdoing is its main operational need. The division's essential mission must be the counteractive action of wrongdoing. Rationale makes it clear that it is ideal to keep a wrongdoing than to put the assets of the division into movement after a wrongdoing has been submitted. Such an operational reaction should bring about an enhanced personal satisfaction for residents, and a diminishment in the dread that is produced by both the truth and view of wrongdoing.

The police office will include the community in the conveyance of its administrations. Unmistakably the police can't be fruitful in accomplishing their main goal without the help and contribution of the general population they serve. Wrongdoing is not exclusively a police issue, and it ought not be considered thusly. Or maybe, wrongdoing must be reacted to as a community issue. In this way, it is imperative for the police office to include the community in its operations. This sharing of obligation includes giving a component to the community to work together with the police both in the identification of community issues and deciding the most suitable techniques for settling them. It is counterproductive for the police to disengage themselves from the community and not enable subjects the chance to work with them.

The police office trusts it must be responsible to the community it serves. The police office likewise is not a substance unto itself. Or maybe, it is a piece of government and exists just with the end goal of serving general society to which it must be responsible. A critical component of responsibility is transparency. Mystery in police work is undesirable as well as outlandish.

Responsibility implies being receptive to the issues and needs of subjects. It additionally implies overseeing police assets in the most savvy way. It must be recollected that the ability to police originates from the assent of those being policed.

The police division is focused on polished methodology in all parts of its operations. The part of the expert association is to serve its customers. The police division must view its part as serving the nationals of the community. An expert association additionally holds fast to a code of morals. The police division must be guided by the Law Enforcement Code of Ethics. A calling polices itself. The police office must guarantee that it keeps up a framework intended to advance the largest amount of teach among its individuals.

The police division will keep up the most astounding norms of trustworthiness. The general public puts resources into its police the most elevated amount of trust. The police, thusly, go into an authoritative game plan with society to maintain that trust. The police should dependably be aware of this authoritative game plan and never disregard that trust. Every individual from the police division must perceive that he or she is held to a higher standard than the private resident. They should perceive that, notwithstanding speaking to the division, they likewise speak to the law enforcement calling and government. They are the personifications of the law. Their lead, both on and taking a break, must be blameless. There must not be even a recognition in people in general's mind that the office's morals are interested being referred to.

Perceiving that society is experiencing gigantic changes, police offices are defied with an awesome test. The substance of that test is to have the capacity to react to issues made by social change, while in the meantime giving the security that holds a general public together amid a time of vulnerability.

By putting forward a reasonable set of qualities, articulating what it has faith in, the police office has an establishment to direct itself. Such an establishment additionally considers authoritative adaptability. What's more, a set of qualities gives the community methods for evaluating its police office without becoming required in specialized operations. Esteem statements fill in as the linkage between the progressing operations of a police division and the community's capacity to take part, as well as to comprehend the purpose behind police office systems.

REFERENCES

https://cops.usdoj.gov/html/dispatch/02-2017/african_americans_in_law_enforcement.asp
https://www.nationaltestingnetwork.com/publicsafetyjobs/
http://www.npdf.org/
https://www.officer.com/
http://www.cityoforlando.net
https://www.policefoundation.org/
https://www.policeone.com/
https://www.trainingreform.org/

Made in the USA
Monee, IL
05 November 2026

67816249R00115